Qutb Minar and its Monuments

Monumental Legacy

Series Editor: Devangana Desai

Monumental Legacy

QUTB MINAR AND
ITS MONUMENTS

B.M. Pande

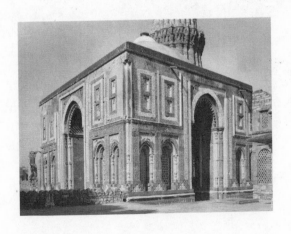

OXFORD
UNIVERSITY PRESS

OXFORD
UNIVERSITY PRESS

It furthers the University's objective of excellence in research, scholarship,
and education by publishing worldwide. Oxford is a registered trademark of
Oxford University Press in the UK and in certain other countries

Published in India by
Oxford University Press
2/11 Ground Floor, Ansari Road, Daryaganj, New Delhi 110 002, India

ISBN-13: 978-0-19-567966-3
ISBN-10: 0-19-567966-0

Typeset in Goudy 11/13.2
by Eleven Arts, Keshav Puram, Delhi 110 035
Printed in India by Replika Press Pvt. Ltd

The publishers, series editor, and authors can accept no responsibility
for any loss or inconvenience caused by any error or misinformation
in the series, though every care is taken in compiling the books.

Series Editor's Preface

There are 812 sites on the World Heritage list, as on July 2005, 'inscribed' as properties by the World Heritage Committee of UNESCO. The list includes, 628 cultural, 160 natural, and 24 mixed sites in 137 States Parties. These are 'considered to be of outstanding value to humanity', and belong to all mankind. The preservation of this shared heritage concerns all of us. India is an active member-state on the World Heritage Forum since 1977, and is one of the countries on the list, with 26 World Heritage Sites. Of these, 21 are recorded as cultural sites, while the rest are natural sites.

I am delighted that the Oxford University Press is publishing brief books on each of the 21 cultural sites, under its series titled Monumental Legacy. So far, the following cultural sites of India have been listed as World Heritage sites:

Ajanta Caves (1983), Ellora Caves (1983), Agra Fort (1983), Taj Mahal (1983), Sun Temple, Konark (1984), Group of Monuments at Mahabalipuram (1985), Churches and Convents of Goa (1986), Group of Monuments at Khajuraho (1986), Group of Monuments at Hampi (1986), Fatehpur Sikri (1986), Group of Monuments at Pattadakal (1987), Elephanta Caves (1987), Brihadisvara Temple, Thanjavur (1987), extended to include under 'Great Living Chola

Temples', Gangaikondacholapuram and Darasuram (2004), Buddhist Monuments at Sanchi (1989), Humayun's Tomb (1993), Qutb Minar and its Monuments (1993), the Darjeeling Himalayan Railway (1999) extended to include under 'Mountain Railways of India', the Nilgiri Mountain Railway (2005), Bodh Gaya (2002), Rock Shelters of Bimbetka (2003), Champaner–Pavagadh Complex (2004), and Chhatrapati Shivaji Terminus, formerly Victoria Terminus (2004).

There is scope, indeed, for recognition of many more Indian sites in future on the World Heritage list. I am sure that as, and when, these are declared as World Heritage Sites, they will be included under the Monumental Legacy series of the Oxford University Press.

The Oxford University Press, in consultation with me, has invited the experts in field to contribute small books, addressed to general readers, on each of these 21 World Heritage Sites in India. These books obviously differ from cheap tourist books and glossy guidebooks and, at the same time, also from specialized monographs. Their importance lies in the fact that they are written by authorities on the subject to enable visitors to see the monuments in proper perspective.

My sincere thanks to all the authors of the series and to the editorial staff at the OUP. Their constant support and enthusiasm are much appreciated.

October 2005   Devangana Desai

Contents

Illustrations

Figures

Photographs

Acknowledgements for permission to reproduce drawings (figures):

Archaeological Survey of India: Figs II–XVI and XIX–XXV; B.R. Mani:
XVII and XVIII

Photograph Credits

American Institute of Indian Studies: 4–7, 9–17, 19–22, and 26;
Rajbir Singh: 1; Author: 2, 3, 8, 18, 23–5, 27–9

Preface and Acknowledgements

I remember my several visits as a child with my father to the Qutb Minar more than fifty years ago on a tonga from Gole Market in New Delhi to Mehrauli. Later, when I grew older, I used to go to the Qutb and other monuments on a bicycle with my friends. The road, from Safdarjung's Tomb to Mehrauli, was lonely and desolate and we were advised to return home before sunset. Later, a bus running on route no. 17, that used to ply rather irregularly between Mehrauli and the Old Delhi Railway Station, became our mode of transport.

Everything has now changed. The tranquility and peace which one experienced while wandering around the Qutb and other monuments in Mehrauli is now missing. There is an almost endless stream of tourists and visitors thronging the Qutb group of monuments—only a few visit the other monuments in its vicinity which are described in this book. Reaching the Qutb is also now much easier than what it used to be some decades ago. One also has to spend more money to reach and visit the Qutb group of monuments. Then there is the Qutb Festival organized by Delhi Tourism, where one can see dance and music performances against the backdrop of the Qutb on the same lines as in some other monuments such as

Khajuraho and Elephanta. The Qutb complex is now also floodlit and open to visitors even after sunset (for which one has to pay more). To me, it seems that the monuments are being turned into commercial ventures; it will be no wonder if some day archaeological monuments are commodified and packaged for tourists rather than simply maintained as part of our heritage and history. Then perhaps there may be a hue and cry to save the monuments and retain their pristine character.

Lest this is taken as an alarmist view, one needs to appreciate that monuments are there to be visited and seen by people without causing any damage to them and, more importantly, maintaining their ambience. This, in my view, can be achieved by exercising control and avoiding overuse or overexposure. The Qutb and its monuments should also be treated accordingly.

This book has been written essentially for tourists and lay visitors. I have followed the format of the other books authored by eminent scholars and published in this series.

I record my gratitude to Devangana Desai for having asked me to write this book and for her patience and perseverance despite the inordinate delay in submission of the manuscript. I have incorporated the suggestions given by her as General Editor of the series; she is known for her erudition and objectivity in all her writings. M.C. Joshi, former Director-General of the Archaeological Survey of India (ASI) and a great scholar, answered my queries and cleared my doubts. I would like to take this opportunity to thank my friends and colleagues in ASI for their ready help. I am particularly grateful to A.K. Sinha, Superintending Archaeologist of the Delhi Circle, Poornima Ray, the ever-helpful and efficient librarian of the Delhi Circle, and Avadhesh Kumar Sharma, incharge of the Qutb Sub-Circle. B.R. Mani, Director, Institute of Archaeology of ASI, was very helpful and kindly allowed me to include and publish the two drawings on Anang Tal and the early Sultanate palace-complex. I would like to thank Kishan Singh, L.S. Mamani and Baldev Singh, my one-time colleagues at ASI, for their help in preparing and finalizing the drawings of plans of monuments and some other text figures included in this book. My old friend Manmohan Bawa, a well-known writer and painter, cartographer, and an inveterate traveller, has drawn the map of Delhi for this book. Ranmal Singh Jhala, a very gifted designer and innovator, and Raj Nath Kaw, formerly of the ASI, helped me in more ways than one. L.T. Khemani provided me with information about Delhi's climate. Rajesh Kochhar, Director, National Institute of Science, Technology, and Development Studies, drew my attention to the article on the proposed identification of the Mehrauli Iron Pillar and also promptly sent me a copy. My friend Bhagwan Singh took time out to listen to some portions while I was writing and rewriting the text. To all of them I owe thanks.

The photographs, except a few, are by Dharam Pal Nanda of the American Institute of Indian Studies (AIIS). Vandana Sinha of AIIS was helpful in many ways. I would like to express my gratitude to them and AIIS for its generosity in supplying the photographs.

My friend José Pereira was constantly reminding me about the book; it is because of his constant cajoling that I was able to complete the book. I would also like to thank Vikas Arya for his help.

The editorial staff at Oxford University Press helped me in several ways for which I am grateful to them.

Finally, I must mention Siddhartha, Shailaja, Mahima, Prabhas, and Swami for their suggestions and help in finalizing the text. My wife was very supportive, as always, while I was writing the book.

I crave the indulgence of scholars for any omissions and mistakes and of tourists and visitors if they find some information wanting.

New Delhi   B.M. Pande
October 2005

Introduction

The Qutb Minar (also spelt as Qutub Minar, Qutab Minar, Kutub Minar, Kutub Meenar) is the most important landmark of Delhi. This despite the fact that Delhi has a large number of historic buildings, monuments, and remains belonging to different periods of history. The Qutb Minar is also the earliest example of a monumental structure in Delhi along with the Quwwat'ul Islam mosque and other buildings and remains within the Qutb complex. Because of its uniqueness and conspicuous appearance, the Qutb Minar and the complex of buildings surrounding it are a must in the itinerary of any visitor to Delhi. Even for those who have seen the Qutb more than once, a visit to the site is always fascinating. The Qutb group of monuments are under the charge of the ASI as centrally-protected monuments of national importance. In the year 1993 this was inscribed as World Heritage site by UNESCO and listed as 'Qutb Minar and its monuments'. The area contiguous to the Qutb to its south has been designated as the Mehrauli Archaeological Park and covers an area of over 40.5 hectares (about 100 acres) of land. It contains over seventy heritage buildings. Among these, some monuments like Jamali Kamali mosque, Balban's tomb, Rajon ki Bain,

Muhammad Quli Khan's tomb, and those in Mehrauli, which are described in this book, are under protection of ASI.

The Qutb is located in south Delhi (**Fig. I**) in an outcrop of the rugged and beautiful Aravalli hills. Well connected by different modes of transport, it is about 15 km (9 miles) from the New Delhi Railway Station, about 20 km ($12^1/_2$ miles) from the Old Delhi Railway Station, and nearly 12 km ($7^1/_2$ miles) from the Nizamuddin Railway Station. Regular buses ply between Mehrauli and these railway stations. The domestic airport is about 15 km (9 miles) from the Qutb while the Indira Gandhi International Airport is about 20 km ($12^1/_2$ miles) away.

The Qutb Minar is in Mehrauli. A village till about the middle of the twentieth century, Mehrauli has now grown into a small town in itself. Historically, Mehrauli has a hoary past. It was in this area that the first-known defence construction in Delhi, known as the Lal Kot, was built by the Tomar ruler Anangpal. The name Mehrauli is derived from Mihirapuri (or Mihirapalli, according to some scholars), suggesting the existence of a sun temple. Mehrauli is also important for the Yogamaya or Jogamaya temple as well as the tomb of Bakhtyar Kaki. A festival called the Phoolwalon ki Sair is held during the month of September–October when fans made of flowers are carried in a colourful procession to the Yogamaya temple as well to the dargah of Bakhtyar Kaki. This area was also known as Yoginipura, due to the presence of a temple dedicated to *yoginis*; the Yogamaya temple perhaps represents the site of an earlier yogini temple. The name Yoginipura occurs in the Palam Baoli inscription dated 1274 CE, as an alternative of Dhilli, an earlier name of Delhi. Dhilli and Yoginipura are also frequently mentioned in Jaina *pattavalis*. In a Jain *vijnaptipatra*, Delhi is mentioned as Dhila-mandala.

While the Qutb Minar dominates the landscape, equally interesting and important are the remains and buildings located in and around the Qutb complex (**Fig. II**). These belong to different periods of Indian history and are of great importance historically as well as from the point of view of the art and architecture of the subcontinent. The site, where the Qutb Minar and other buildings marking the establishment of Islamic rule over northern India are

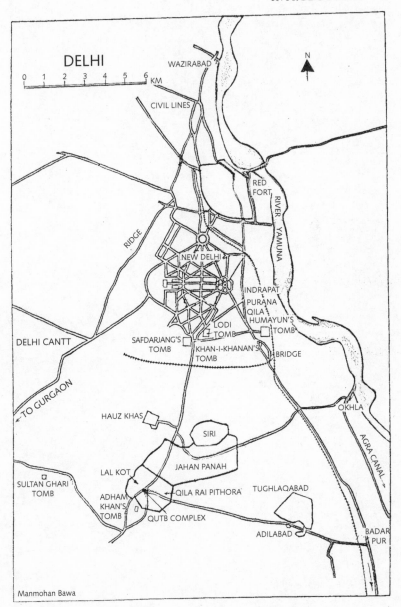

Fig. I. Map of Delhi showing some important monuments

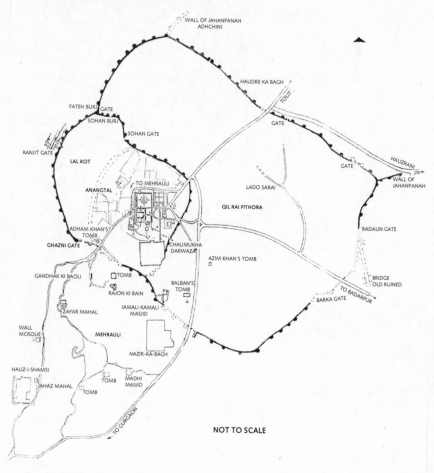

Fig. II. Qutb Minar and its monuments (not to scale)

located, was once the citadel of the Tomars and the Chauhans, represented by the ruins of Lal Kot and Qila Rai Pithora, respectively. Besides Lal Kot, there are other remains in the vicinity of the Qutb Minar. Traditionally, the site also represents the first city of Delhi, however, new archaeological discoveries have provided evidence of the remains of earlier periods. In the Qutb complex also stands the Iron Pillar, famous for having withstood more than sixteen centuries without showing any signs of deterioration. This pillar is also important for the fourth-century inscription engraved on it. Ruins of temples, tombs, and dargahs, *baolis* or stepwells, *hauz* or tank, fortification walls, palaces, madrasas, *sarai*, orchards, mosques, etc., belonging to different periods, all set within a rugged landscape, have lent a distinct character to the area. Equally interesting are structures like the seventeenth-century octagonal tomb of Muhammad Quli Khan, renovated and used as a residence by Sir Charles Theophilus Metcalfe, Resident at the Mughal court. Metcalfe also erected structures in pseudo-Mughal style as well as stepped pyramidal towers locally called *garhgaj*; all these are known as Metcalfe's follies.

The Mehrauli village—now overgrown like most other Delhi villages—still retains some of its original character. The Yogamaya temple is adjacent to the Qutb complex, on the way to Mehrauli. Further beyond the Yogamaya temple, one can see Adham Khan's tomb and head straight for the Dargah Qutb Sahib. Just outside the western entrance of the dargah is Zafar Mahal, built by Akbar II (1806–37), where the last Mughal emperor, Bahadur Shah II (popularly known as Bahadur Shah Zafar) (1837–57) carried out certain changes and reconstructions. Other significant remains in the vicinity include the Hauz-i-Shamsi, Jahaz Mahal, Rajon ki Bain, Gandhak ki Baoli, and Jamali Kamali's mosque and tomb.

The Qutb complex (**Photo 1**) mainly comprises of the Quwwatu'l Islam mosque with its extensions and the screens, the Qutb Minar, 'Ala'i Darwaza, 'Ala'i Minar, Iltutmish's tomb, 'Alau'd-Din Khalji's tomb and madrasa, and the Iron Pillar within the mosque quadrangle. Adjacent to, but outside the 'Ala'i Darwaza, is the tomb of Imam Zamin. The other monuments which the visitor can see are some late Mughal gateways, a sarai, and a mosque. In the lawns of the Qutb

Photo 1. View of Quwwatu'l Islam Masjid, and its later extensions and 'Ala'i Minar, from the Qutb Minar

complex is also kept the cupola which had been placed atop the Qutb Minar in the nineteenth century but was brought down in 1848 because it looked incongruous.

The monuments and archaeological remains in the Qutb area thus represent different periods of Indian history. Anangpal II built the Lal Kot between 1052 and 1060 CE. The citadel and fortification of the Tomars and the Chauhans, who ruled over Delhi from about the tenth century to the twelfth century, the pillars and architectural components reused in the Quwwatu'l Islam mosque and later buildings, remains of the later Mughal period as represented by the

gateways of the sarai and mosque, the tomb of Imam Zamin who came to India from Turkestan during the reign of Sikandar Lodi (1488–1517) or the seventeenth-century tomb of Muhammad Quli Khan used as a residence by Metcalfe, etc., represent the legacy of several centuries.

ONE

Archaeological and
Historical Background

U ntil a few decades ago, the Qutb area was mentioned as the first city—out of the seven cities of Delhi—as represented by the walls of Lal Kot and the Qila Rai Pithora **(Fig. II)**. However, Delhi's past goes back to much earlier times. This is evident from the discovery of prehistoric stone tools in areas contiguous to the Qutb, both to its north in the campus of the Jawaharlal Nehru University and towards its south-east, in and around Anangpur and beyond in the Aravallis. The stone tools found at these sites mainly comprise hand axes and cleavers made of fine-grained quartzite and assigned to the Late Acheulian phase of the Lower Palaeolithic or Early Stone Age besides some microliths ascribed to the Mesolithic or the Middle Stone Age. The Qutb area, being in the Aravallis, may also yield similar remains. Thereafter, we have evidence of Chalcolithic and Iron Age settlements. These are represented by ancient mounds in different areas of Delhi; Bhorgarh near Narela in north Delhi and Mandoli in east Delhi have provided evidence of occupation of these sites going back to Late Harappan times (which is placed sometime in the second millennium BCE). Archaeological excavations at these sites have shown that these were also inhabited during subsequent periods. Bhorgarh was inhabited during the Painted Grey Ware

(PGW) (first millennium BCE), Kushan (second–third centuries CE), and Mughal (sixteenth-seventeenth centuries CE) periods, while at Mandoli the last occupation was during the Gupta period (fourth–fifth centuries CE).

Remains of Early Iron Age settlements dateable to about 1100–800 BCE as represented by the PGW have also been found elsewhere in Delhi. Apart from Bhorgarh and Mandoli, mentioned above, some of the other sites which have yielded this characteristic ware are—ancient mound inside the Purana Qila and Salimgarh, Khera Kalan, Kharkhari Nahar, Jhatikara, etc. The site of the Purana Qila, according to tradition, represents Indraprastha, the capital of the Pandavas that lay in Khandavaprastha. Archaeological excavations of the ancient mound, enclosed by the walls of the sixteenth-century citadel, have yielded remains of the Late Mughal (late eighteenth–early nineteenth centuries), Early Mughal (sixteenth century), Sultanate (1206–1526 CE), Rajput (c. 900–1200 CE), Post-Gupta (c. 700–800 CE), Gupta (c. 400–600 CE), Shaka-Kushan (c. 100 BCE–300 CE), Shunga (c. 200–100 BCE), and Maurya (c. third century BCE) periods. The discovery of an Ashokan rock edict near East of Kailash shows the direct association of the Maurya emperor Ashoka with Delhi besides suggesting that Delhi was on the ancient trunk route which connected different commercial centres and provincial capitals. Seen in the context of the remains of the Maurya period from Purana Qila excavations, it also confirms the importance of Delhi in ancient times.

While archaeological excavations and other discoveries have pushed back the antiquity of Delhi to pretty early times, Delhi became the seat of power and remained so almost continuously from about the late twelfth century onwards with its capture by Qutbu'd-Din Aibak. Prior to this, Delhi was under the Chahamana or the Chauhan dynasty. King Vigraharaja IV (c.1153–64 CE), also known as Visaladeva or Bisaldeo, of this dynasty captured the city from the Tomars. The exploits of Bisaldeo are recorded in an inscription engraved on the Ashokan pillar at Kotla Firoz Shah.

The area was earlier under the Tomar Rajputs whose vestiges are represented by their citadel known as the Lal Kot (Fig. III). The Tomars were the feudatories of the Pratiharas and had gained control over Delhi sometime in the eighth century. There is a strong bardic

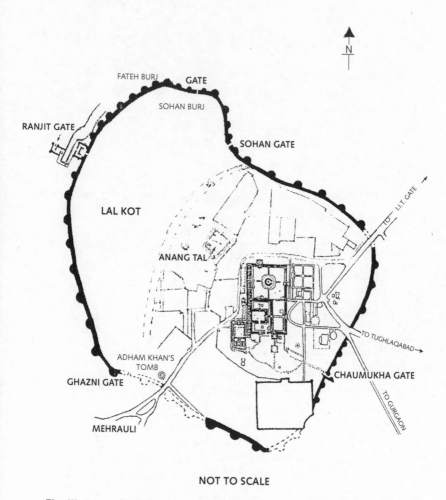

NOT TO SCALE

Fig. III. Map of Lal Kot (not to scale)

tradition about the Tomars with reference to Delhi. The reservoir known as Suraj Kund, located about 11 km (7 miles) from the Qutb to the south-east of Tughluqabad, is traditionally ascribed to King Surajpal of the Tomar dynasty whose historical identity is not certain. Again, the Anangpur (or Arangpur) dam is ascribed to Anangpal of the same dynasty who is mentioned in *Prithvirajaraso* as the founder of Delhi. Anangpal, whose dates are variously given as either middle of the eighth or middle of the eleventh century, also built Lal Kot as well as the Anang Tal just behind the Yogamaya temple. According to tradition, the Iron Pillar is also believed to have been brought by Anangpal who had had it installed in its present location within the Quwwatu'l Islam mosque. Not much remains of this citadel except some ramparts built of stone rubble and the moat of which only some traces can be seen. The walls of the rampart vary between 3 m (10 feet) and 9 m (29$^1/_2$ feet) in thickness. (Lal Kot and Anang Tal have been subjected to archaeological excavations by the ASI.) The present Qutb area is enclosed at places by the walls of Lal Kot and their subsequent extension during the Khalji period.

The history of the area is known with greater certainty with the capture of Delhi in 1192 CE by Qutbu'd-Din Aibak (Qutb al-Din Aibak), the slave of Muhammad bin Sam (Muhammad ibn Sam) of Ghur (in Afghanistan). Muhammad bin Sam, more popularly known as Muhammad Ghuri or Ghori, defeated Prithiviraja II, the Chauhan ruler, in 1192 CE in the second battle of Tarain in Haryana. In 1206 CE, Qutbu'd-Din declared himself the Sultan of Delhi after the death of Muhammad bin Sam. With this, Delhi became the capital of the Mamluk or Slave dynasty. Qutbu'd-Din built the Quwwatu'l Islam mosque and also laid the foundation of the Qutb Minar within Lal Kot and Qila Rai Pithora. Qutbu'd-Din's successor was his son-in-law, Shamsu'd-Din Iltutmish (1211–36 CE). He extended the Quwwatu'l Islam mosque and also completed the Qutb Minar. Iltutmish, whose tomb is located close to the Quwwatu'l Islam mosque, is also credited with the construction of Sultan Ghari's tomb which is among the earliest monumental Muslim tombs in India. This tomb was built in 1231 CE for Iltutmish's eldest son and heir-apparent Nasiru'd-Din Mahmud who died sometime in 1228 or 1229 CE. Located on the

Mehrauli-Palam road, Sultan Ghari's tomb is worth a visit. Iltutmish was succeeded by his eldest son Ruknu'd-Din Firuz Shah even though he had nominated his daughter Raziya to succeed him. Ruknu'd-Din Firuz Shah could rule only for six months and Raziya became the Sultan of Delhi in 1236 CE. After her assasination in 1240 CE, 'Alau'd-Din Masud and Nasiru'd-Din Mahmud came to power. There being no heir to Nasiru'd-Din, he was succeeded by Balban, one of the slaves of Iltutmish. Balban ruled from 1265 to 1287 CE. A highly dilapidated domeless building, not very far from the Qutb, is generally believed to be Balban's tomb. This monument is well worth a visit, being the first Indo-Islamic building in which a true arch has been employed. The Mamluk dynasty lasted up to 1290, when the Khaljis captured Delhi from Shamsu'd-Din Kaimurth who had succeeded Kaiqubad when he was killed at Kilokari on the banks of the Yamuna.

The Khaljis, although from Afghanistan, were originally Turks. 'Alau'd-Din Khalji ascended the throne in 1296 and ruled up to 1316. He is better known among the six Khalji rulers because of his political exploits as well as architectural works. Among these, his tomb and the madrasa, the elegant gateway called the 'Ala'i Darwaza, and the unfinished 'Ala'i Minar, are all located within the Qutb complex. 'Alau'd-Din also extended the existing Quwwatu'l Islam mosque and carried out some repairs to the Qutb Minar. In 1303, he laid the foundation of Siri, the second city of Delhi. He also built, in, 1305, the large tank called Hauz-i-'Ala'i—now known as Hauz-Khas—to meet the requirements of the inhabitants of Siri. The Shahpur Jat village and Khel Gaon (built during the 1982 Asiad Games) are located in what was originally Siri.

Khalji rule lasted only for four years after 'Alau'd-Din's death. The last Khalji ruler was Mubarak Shah, who was beheaded by Khusraw Khan in a palace coup. In September 1320, Ghazi Malik defeated Khusraw Khan and assumed the title of Ghiyasu'd-Din Tughluq and became the first Tughluq sultan of Delhi. Ghiyasu'd-Din Tughluq built a new walled city at Tughluqabad, the third city of Delhi. His successor, Muhammad bin Tughluq, enjoyed a period of long rule from 1325 to 1351. He founded the fourth city of Delhi, Jahanpanah, which he provided with a walled enclosure. He also built the fortress of Adilabad to the south of Tughlaqabad fort. Muhammad bin Tughluq carried out some repairs to the Qutb Minar in 1332 after it was damaged in an earthquake.

The next Tughluq ruler, Firuz Shah (1351–88 CE), was a prolific builder, with an interest in old buildings and other remains. He made a new capital called Firuzabad, which is the fifth city of Delhi. The present Kotla Firoz Shah represents this city. Among other things, Firuz Shah also brought two Ashokan pillars to Delhi, one of which was erected atop the tall pyramidal structure at Kotla. He carried out repairs at Sultan Ghari's tomb, Suraj Kund and, more importantly, Qutb Minar, where he restored two upper stories that had collapsed in an earthquake. This fact is recorded in an inscription engraved by the workers who carried out the repairs at the Qutb.

Firuz Shah Tughluq's death in 1388 was followed by instability even though the Tughluqs continued to rule up to 1414. Timur's invasion in 1398 as well as political instability finally led to the governor of Punjab, Khizr Khan, declaring himself the ruler and founder of the Sayyid dynasty in 1414. The Sayyids lasted for thirty years, during which there were four rulers. Except for some tombs, no significant architectural activity seems to have taken place during the Sayyid rule. In 1451, 'Alau'd-Din Alam Shah, the last Sayyid ruler, was dethroned when Buhlul Lodi, the Afghan governor of Sirhind, captured the throne and established the Lodi dynasty.

Buhlul Lodi ruled from 1451 to 1489. He was followed by Sikandar (1489–1517 CE) and Ibrahim Lodi (1517–26 CE). The tomb of Imam Zamin, adjacent to the 'Ala'i Darwaza in the Qutb complex, was built during the reign of Sikandar Lodi. There are several other buildings of the Lodi period mainly comprising tombs and mosques which are located in the Lodi Garden in New Delhi. In 1526, Babur defeated and killed Ibrahim Lodi in the battle of Panipat.

The establishment of Mughal rule by Babur (1526–30 CE) marks an important phase in the history of India particularly from the point of view of art and architecture. Babur, however, did not make Delhi his capital. He ruled from Agra where he died in 1530. His son Humayun succeeded him. He was defeated twice (1539, 1540) by Sher Khan, an Afghan from Sur. Assuming the title of Sher Shah, he ruled briefly from 1540 to 1545 CE. Sher Shah possessed exceptional qualities. In the brief period that he reigned, he adopted various administrative and fiscal measures of far-reaching significance, undertook various works including construction of roads—the Grand Trunk Road being one of these, provided with facilities like sarais and several forts, tombs, and mosques. The Grand Trunk Road was originally from Attock to Delhi but was later extended to Sonargaon near Dhaka. In Delhi, Sher Shah built the Purana Qila and a town around it which marks the sixth city of Delhi. Inside the Purana Qila is the Qal'a-i-Kuhna Masjid and the Sher Mandal, an octagonal double-storeyed tower; the Qal'a-i-Kuhna Masjid is considered to be an important development in mosque architecture in India. After Sher Shah's death in 1545 at Kalinjar in Banda district, Uttar Pradesh, his son Islam Shah, who is also known as Salim Shah, succeeded him and ruled till 1554. The Salimgarh Fort, adjoining the Red Fort to its north, and 'Isa Khan's tomb are ascribed to him. Islam Shah was succeeded by Sikandar Shah. Sur rule came to an end when Sikander Shah was defeated by Humayun in July 1555.

Humayun, however, did not survive for long, succumbing to injuries caused by a fall from the steps of Sher Mandal in January 1556. He too had planned a city, having laid its foundations in 1533 during his first stint as ruler. Called Dinpanah, it was destroyed by Sher Shah Sur; Humayun himself had had the building material robbed from Siri, the city built by 'Alau'd-Din Khalji. (Siri suffered the same fate again when it was levelled to the ground to build the Asiad village in 1982.) More important is the Jamali Kamali Masjid, not far from the Qutb, which was completed during his period. Humayun's tomb was built later by his widow and is one of the finest examples of Mughal architecture. The tomb was inscribed as World Heritage by UNESCO in 1993.

Akbar (1556–1605 CE), the elder son of Humayun, succeeded him at the tender age of 13. He built a new town at Fatehpur Sikri, about 40 km (25 miles) west of Agra, and the Agra Fort. Since he continued to rule from Agra, he did not erect any buildings in Delhi. He is credited, however, with the erection of *kos-minars* along the Grand Trunk Road and other minor roads of the Mughal Empire. The tomb of Adham Khan in Mehrauli was built during his reign in 1562. Jahangir (1605–27 CE), who succeeded Akbar, also did not contribute to building activity in Delhi notwithstanding his eclectic interests. Khan-i-Khanan's tomb and Chaunsath Khamba are the two buildings of his period. Some sarais are attributed to his period as well.

Shah Jahan's reign (1628–58 CE) marks a period of prolific activity in the domain of art and architecture. He used marble in his buildings and decorated these with pietra dura or inlay work. He added new buildings within the Lahore and Agra forts and in other places. The crowning achievement of Shah Jahan's architectural activity is, of course, the Taj Mahal in Agra, the construction of which began in 1632 and took seventeen years. In 1638, Shah Jahan transferred his capital from Agra to Delhi. Here he laid the foundation of Shahjahanabad, the seventh city of Delhi. The Lal Qila or Red Fort with various palaces and other buildings inside, the Jami' Masjid, the city wall, and various gates are some of the prominent monuments which form part of the walled city of Shahjahanabad. During this period were built the Fatehpuri Masjid at the western end of Chandni Chowk by Fatehpuri Begam, and the tombs of his daughters Jahanara and Raushanara.

Unlike his father, Aurangzeb (1658–1707 CE) was not so keen on such pursuits. He remained preoccupied with military campaigns and lived a spartan life. The only architectural work of his period in Delhi is the Moti Masjid (Pearl Mosque) inside the Red Fort.

The disintegration of the Mughal Empire began with Aurangzeb's death in 1707. The rulers who followed are generally referred to as the Later Mughals. They were: Bahadur Shah I (1707–12), Jahandar Shah (1712–13), Farrukhsiyar (1713–19), Muhammad Shah (1719–48), Ahmad Shah (1748–54), Alamgir II (1754–9), Shah Alam (1759–1806), Akbar II (1806–37), and, finally, Bahadur Shah II (1837–57). Internal dissensions, repeated onslaughts of foreign invaders and other Indian rulers, and finally the entrenchment of foreign powers eroded the authority of the Later Mughals and they were reduced to the position of nominal rulers. The impoverished kingdom of ineffective rulers could not indulge in architectural pursuits like their predecessors. The only two buildings of note from this period are the tomb of Safdar Jang (1739–54) built in AH 1167 (1753–4 CE) and the observatory popularly but inappropriately known as Jantar Mantar erected by Maharaja Jai Singh II of Jaipur (1699–1743 CE) sometime in 1724. The Later Mughals were gradually losing their effective control even in the Red Fort. This led to their efforts to shift elsewhere in Delhi and they found Mehrauli suitable for the purpose. As a result, nearly all Later Mughal buildings are found in Mehrauli. The sarai along with the mosque within, another smaller mosque close by—all within the Qutb complex—Zafar Mahal built by Akbar II near the western entrance of the Dargah Qutb Sahib, the small Moti Masjid built sometime in 1709 by Bahadur Shah I, and the gateways erected by Farrukhsiyar within the dargah complex in Mehrauli represent the building activity of the Later Mughals.

The seizure of power by the British in 1858 marks the beginning of what is termed the Modern Period. Most buildings of the early phase of British rule are located in north Delhi between Kashmiri Gate and Kingsway Camp. With the shifting of the capital from Calcutta to Delhi in 1911, foundation was laid for the construction of New Delhi with its sprawling bungalows, the new Secretariat and other buildings, the Viceregal Lodge (now the Rashtrapati Bhawan), and various well-laid out roads and avenues, all within what was called the Delhi Imperial Zone. It was in this period that the process of exposing archaéological remains, and the restoration and conservation of monuments within the Qutb complex and elsewhere started. At the same time, some of the monuments in the Qutb area were also reused or new structures erected; the Metcalfe's follies or Major Smith's cupola which was placed atop the Qutb Minar belong to this period.

TWO

Monuments—The Qutb Complex

Late Mughal Sarai

The approach to the group of monuments within the Qutb complex (**Figs IV and V**) is from the east through a gateway that originally formed part of a sarai. Opposite it stands the western gateway (**Photo 2**) of the sarai, remains of which are extant on the northern side. The southern half of the sarai and traces of a Late Mughal garden to its west, being in a highly ruinous condition, were dismantled in the second decade of the twentieth century when large-scale conservation works were carried out in the Qutb complex. The sarai follows the usual plan of sarais built during the Mughal period along the Grand Trunk Road. The extant remains of the sarai consist of a row of arched compartments on the north and the east and a mosque, besides the two gateways facing each other on the east and the west. The arched compartments on either side of the entrance gateways and the garden are no longer extant. The sarai, along with its two gateways and the mosque, belongs to the Late Mughal period and may have been built along with the other buildings in Mehrauli when the Later Mughals shifted here.

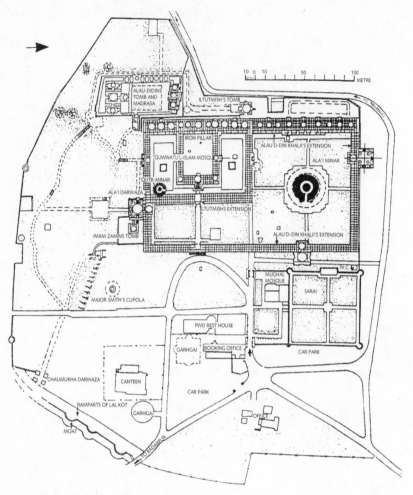

Fig. IV. Qutb archaeological area (not to scale)

Fig. V. Conjectural restoration of Qutb complex. From J.A. Page

Photo 2. Western gateway of late Mughal sarai

Quwwatu'l Islam Masjid

The Qutb Minar, which dominates the landscape, was built in 1199 CE as an adjunct of the Quwwatu'l Islam Masjid **(Fig. VI; Photo 3)**. The Quwwatu'l Islam—meaning the 'Might of Islam'—mosque is built on the plinth of an earlier temple. It can be approached from the east by a descending flight of steps leading to an entrance doorway. On the inner lintel of this doorway is an inscription of Qutbu'd-Din Aibak in Arabic and in what is known as Naskh (or Naskhi) script, recording the demolition of twenty-seven temples, the materials of which were used in the construction of the mosque. These temples were both Brahmanical as well as Jain and, as the inscription records, were built at a cost of 20 lakh coins each. The inscription quotes verses 91–2 from Surah III of the Quran, followed by the text as under:

This fort was conquered and this Jami'-Masjid was built in (the months of) the year 587 [1191–2 CE] by the Amir, the great and glorious commander of the army, (named) Qutbu'd-daulatwa'd-Din, the Amiru'l-umara Aibak Sultani, may God strengthen his helpers. The materials of 27 temples, on (the erection

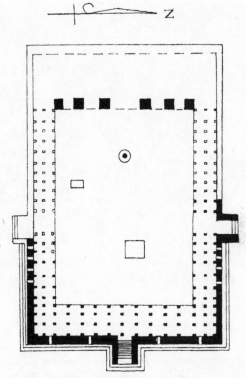

Fig. VI. Quwwatu'l Islam Masjid, plan (not to scale)

of) each of which 2,000,000 Deliwals had been spent, were used in (the construction of) this mosque. May God the great and glorious have mercy on him who should pray for the faith of the founder of the good (building).

Significantly, in the inscription, Qutbu'd-Din Aibak mentions it as Jami' Masjid and not Quwwatu'l Islam Masjid. Another inscription in the arch typanum of the eastern gateway reads: 'This mosque was built by Qutbu'd-Din Aibak. May God have mercy on him who should pray for the faith of the founder of this good (building).'

Qutbu'd-Din began building the Quwwatu'l Islam mosque in 1192 soon after annexing Delhi. It was completed in 1197–8 CE as is clear from the inscription, in Naskh characters, on the arch tympanum of the northern gateway. The inscription, preceded by verse 26 from

Photo 3. Quwwatu'l Islam Masjid, with Iron Pillar in foreground

Surah X of the Quran, records: 'In (the months of) the year [five hundred] and ninety-two [1197–8 CE] this building was erected by the high order of the exalted Sultan Muizzu'd-dunya-wa'd-Din Muhammad-ibn-Sam, the helper of the prince of the faithful'. It is thus the earliest surviving mosque in India save for the pre-Sultanate monuments in Kachch (Kutch) in Gujarat.

The mosque is built over a high plinth or platform and comprises a rectangular court measuring 65.2m (214 feet) by 45.4 m (149 feet). It is enclosed by cloisters or pillared verandahs in which the carved pillars, lintels, ceiling slabs, and other architectural members of the aforementioned twenty-seven Brahmanical and Jain temples have been used. The colonnade or the pillared verandah has, on the eastern side, a triple row of pillars while the extant northern and southern sides have double row. The prayer chamber on the west is four bays deep. At the corners of the mosque, intermediate storeys or mezzanine floors were raised for female worshippers. Entry into the mosque was from the three colonnaded sides with each entrance having a porch. The circular ceiling just behind the entrance doorway on the eastern side as well as the intermediate storeys still preserve examples of ornamental temple ceilings. There are several sculptures, ornamental

motifs, and beautifully carved figures in almost each pillar or bracket
(Photo 4), most of them having been damaged due to deliberate
disfiguring. One can see in these pillars typical ornamental motifs
like the chain-and-bell, *ghata-pallava* or pot from which emanate
flowers, endless knots, creepers, lotus flowers, and many other motifs
(Photos 5 and 6). The intermediate storey on the south-eastern
end of the cloister has well-preserved lintels depicting scenes from
the life of the Jain *Tirthankaras* and various Jain deities. In fact, there
exists a tradition among Jains that there was originally a temple
dedicated to the Jain Tirthankara Parshvanatha at the site of the
Quwwatu'l Islam mosque. It is also said that this temple was built
prior to 1132 by Sahu Nattal, an Agrawal, who was a minister in the
court of the Tomar ruler Anangpal III. This is also indicated by the
poet Shridhara in his *Parshva Purana*. The presence of Jain sculptures,
temple pillars, etc. in the mosque lend some credence to this tradition.
This tradition also mentions, interestingly enough, that this temple
was located in the middle of a tank. It may perhaps be worthwhile to
explore the possibility of the existence of the tank notwithstanding
the large-scale works executed in the second decade of the twentieth
century. One of the sculptured lintels, which has been placed over a
window opening in the north façade of the mosque, shows the birth
of Krishna and some related events. In one of the pillars—hewn out
of quartzite—on the southern side one can clearly see a seated
Tirthankara figure. Besides these, Brahmanical and Jain sculptures
have also been found from the Qutb area which represent the spoils
of temples existing here earlier. Among these may be mentioned
the beautiful four-armed Vishnu image bearing the date *Samvat* 1204
(1147 CE); this sculpture is now on display at the National Museum,
New Delhi. The ASI has in its collection a square pillar carved in
quartzite having on each of its three faces a seated Tirthankara figure;
the fourth face has Ganesha who, in the Jain tradition, is the
harbinger of prosperity and *kalyana* or well-being. While it is difficult
to identify each of the Tirthankaras, one of these seems to be the
figure of Rishabhanatha.

It is interesting to note the masons' marks engraved on some of
the pillars used in the Quwwatu'l Islam mosque. The bases, shafts,
and capitals were originally numbered in some cases while one pillar-

Photo 4. Quwwatu'l Islam Masjid, temple pillar with brackets

Photo 5. Quwwatu'l Islam Masjid, temple pillar showing different motifs

Photo 6. Quwwatu'l Islam Masjid, temple pillar

shaft had the word *Kachal* engraved in Nagari characters on one side and the date (Vikrama Samvat) 1124 (1067 CE) on the other which corresponds to the time of Anangpal, the founder of Lal Kot. The other masons' marks give the direction, position, and number of the architectural members.

After completion of the mosque in 1197–8, a large stone screen was erected on the western side. It consists of a massive central arch rising to height of 16 m (52 feet 6 inches) and width of 6.7 m (22 feet), and two smaller arches on either side of the central arch which have the same shape as the central one.

The ogee-shaped arches of the screen are not true arches and have been built by corbelling. At the apex, stones have been placed in the manner of voussoirs to give the semblance of an arch. This is because the artisans and masons engaged for the work were perhaps more familiar with this method of construction. The beautifully ornamented screen consists of borders of inscriptions and geometrical and arabesque designs. The hand of Hindu craftsmen can be clearly seen in the serpentine tendrils, undulating leaves of its scroll-work, and in the fine characters of the Quranic inscriptions. An incomplete inscription on the south pier at the foot of the inscribed band framing the central arch states: '...date, the 20th of Zil Qada of the year five hundred and ninety-four [1199 CE]'. Another inscription on one of the pillars in Aibak's prayer chamber reads: 'Under the supervision [*mutavalli*-ship] of the slave Fazl ibn Abil Ma'ali.'

The Quwwatu'l Islam Masjid was enlarged twice by two later rulers **(Figs IV and V)**. It was first enlarged in 1230 CE by Shamsu'd-Din Iltutmish (1211–36 CE), the son-in-law of Qutbu'd-Din, who doubled its size by extending the colonnades, the screen arches and the prayer hall beyond and outside the original enclosure. An inscription on the south end pier (east face) of the southern arch of Iltutmish's southern extension of the great screen reads: '...in (the months of) the year six hundred and twenty-seven [1229 CE]'. While the arches of the screen built by Iltutmish are still corbelled, the inscriptions and the ornamentation are clearly different from the original screens built by Qutbu'd-Din Aibak and are Saracenic in character. It has been suggested that, 'Iltutmish brought in skilled calligraphers from Iran, particularly to design the intricate panels with the traditional cursive Naskhi.'

Photo 7. Iron Pillar,
details of top portion

The Qutb Minar, which was outside
the original enclosure of the mosque, now
became a part of the extended mosque
enclosure.

The mosque was enlarged again by
Alau'd-Din Khalji (1296–1316 CE). This
extension nearly doubled the area of the
mosque. Alau'd-Din Khalji also provided
'two gateways on the longer eastern side
and one each on the north and south.'
The gateway on the south side is known
as 'Ala'i Darwaza and was erected in
AH 710 1310–11 CE. The screen arches
which Alau'd-Din had planned could not
be built as is evident from the remains of
eight piers on the western side to the north
of the screen arches of Iltutmish. Alaud'-
Din had also planned a minar right in the
centre of the north court. Called the Ala'i-
Minar, it also remained unfinished.

Iron Pillar

In front of the great screen, in the courtyard
of the mosque, is the Iron Pillar with an
inscription in three stanzas comprising
six lines engraved on its northern face.
The inscription is in Sanskrit in the Gupta
script and can be ascribed to the fourth
century CE on palaeographic grounds.
The pillar comprises a shaft—7.21 m (23
feet 8 inches) in length of which 0.51 m
(1 foot 8 inches) is buried below the
ground—having a smooth surface barring
the lower portion which has a rough surface
caused by hammer marks. The top portion

of the pillar has a capital with seven components (**Photo 7**) comprising, from bottom to top, 'fluted inverted-lotus bell structure, the slanted rod structure, three rounded discs with serrated edges, a circular disc, and finally the box pedestal.' On the top of the pedestal is a circular slab having a rectangular-shaped slot or hole with one end pointed where perhaps some figure or object was fixed. This can be inferred from the inscription which mentions the pillar as Vishnu-*dhvaja* or the standard of Vishnu erected on the Vishnupadagiri, that is, the hill located at the feet of Vishnu or the hill bearing the feet of Vishnu.

The inscription (**Photo 8**) records the exploits of a king Chandra who can be identified with Chandragupta II (375–414 CE) of the Gupta dynasty. The following is the translation of the original text of the inscription:

[Verse 1] On whose arm fame was inscribed by the sword, when, in battle in the Vanga territory, he dashed back with his breast the enemies who, uniting together, came upon (him); by whom crossing the seven mouths of the Sindhu the Vahlikas were

Photo 8. Iron Pillar, Gupta inscription

conquered in battle; by the breezes of whose valour the southern ocean is still perfumed;

[Verse 2] Who, the king, quitting this *go* [earth], as if dejected, has resorted to another go [intermediate region]; who, though he has in his body, gone to the land [*avani*] conquered for [religious] rites, has remained on (*kshiti*) [earth] by fame; [and] whose great *pratapa* [valour], [though it is now] the conclusion of the exertion of [him] who had destroyed his enemies, does not as yet leave the earth like the *pratapa* [heat] of the conflagration in a great forest [though it has now] subsided;

[Verse 3] by that king, who acquired sole supreme sovereignty on earth by his own arm and for very long [and] who having the name Chandra and bearing beauty of face like that of the full moon, with devotion having fixed [his] mind upon Vishnu, this lofty flag staff of the divine Vishnu was set up on the hill, Vishnupada.

There are also some later inscriptions engraved on the pillar. An important inscription, in Nagari, records '*Samvat Dihali 1109 Ang Pal bahi*' meaning—in Samvat 1109 (1052–3 CE) Ang Pal (that is, Anangpal) founded Delhi. An alternate reading of this inscription is '*Sammat Dhilli 1109 Amgapala vadi*'; the meaning, however, is the same.) This obviously refers to Anangpal, the Tomar king who is credited as being the founder of Delhi. That the iron pillar was located in the temple here is also suggested by an inscription in one of the pillars of the colonnade, bearing the date (Vikrama) Samvat 1124 (1067 CE).

Later inscriptions bear the date AH 964 (1556 CE), Samvat 1572 (1515 CE), 1580 (1523 CE), 1767 (1710 CE), 1883 (1826 CE), and 1888 (1831–2 CE). Among these later inscriptions, the one giving the name of Anangpal is important since it refers to the Tomar king as the founder of Delhi.

The other inscription of Samvat 1883 (1826 CE), even though much later in date, also provides interesting information, although historically inaccurate. It records the visit of Chhatra Singhaji Chauhan in Samvat 1883 and mentions that 'Prithiraj (flourished) in Samvat 1151' and that 'in the twenty-third generation from him was descended the illustrious Maharava ji Chhatrasingha ji...'. Another inscription recounts that 'in Samvat 419, there was a Raja, a scion of the Tuvar (Tomara) race named Amgapal, and in Sammat (that is, Samvat) 648 a certain Vasudeva Chauhan Raja Indra. In the twenty-first generation from the latter was Raja Prithiraja in Samvat 1151 and in the twenty-eighth generation from him Raja Chatrasingh in Samvat 1888. The only fact of any value supplied by these inscriptions is the date of Samvat 1109 for Anangpal. The rest of the information, having been recorded from memory in the years 1827 and 1832 is incorrect. The most glaring mistake that is at once spotted is the date of Samvat 1151 (1096 CE) for Prithiraj. Besides these later Nagari inscriptions, a short Persian epigraph dated AH 964 (1556 CE) records the name of a certain Ali Asghar Husain, son of Israel.

It has been suggested that the Iron Pillar is not in situ and was brought from some other site. This is because of lack of any other evidence in the form of remains in the area that could be dated to the fourth century CE. According to bardic tradition, the pillar was brought here by Anangpal. Some scholars have hazarded a guess about the pillar being located originally in Mathura. In a recent study, it has been proposed that the pillar was originally located at Udayagiri, near Vidisha, in Madhya Pradesh, where it was fixed atop the hill famous for the rock-cut caves and bas reliefs of Vaishnava, Shaiva, and Jain affiliation as well as the plinth of a temple of the Gupta period (319–600 CE). Vishnupadagiri, mentioned in the inscription, has been identified on the basis of literary, numismatic, and geographic evidences with Udayagiri. While it was hitherto believed that the iron pillar was a Garuda-dhvaja, that is, staff surmounted by Garuda, it has been suggested that it was a chakra-dhvaja and the object atop the capital of the pillar was a chakra or circular disc having a diameter of 0.508 m (20 inches). The Iron Pillar, it has been hypothesized, was probably located in the entrance to the main complex at Udayagiri facing the east. It therefore had astronomical significance in view of the fact that Udayagiri is located on the tropic of Cancer.

Made of pure malleable iron and with hardly any signs of rusting, despite the fact that it is more than 1600 years old, the pillar is a fine example of ancient Indian metallurgical and engineering skill. While its tapering shaft is smooth, its base is knobby, with small pieces of iron which have been inserted to tie it to the foundation and a lead sheet to cover the portion below the present floor-level. 'It is a classic product of forge welding technique employed by ancient Indians to manufacture large iron objects.' In this process, iron lumps 'were obtained by the solid state reduction of iron ore in the presence of charcoal' and were forged together in the form of a pillar. On the basis of metallurgical analysis it seems that the pillar was manufactured by using vertical forging technique while the finish was given by placing it in a horizontal position. Weighing about 6100 kg, the pillar contains 99.72 per cent iron.

It might interest visitors to know certain facts about the dimensions of the pillar and the relative proportions of its different portions and components. In the late 1950s and early 1960s, the following dimensions of the pillar were recorded:

Distance from bottom of the pillar to the level of the yard	0.48 m (1 foot 7 inches)
Height of the yard level to the raised platform	0. 46 m (1 foot 6 inches)
Height of the cylindrical portion above ground level	5. 18 m (17 feet)
Height of the decorated portion	1. 04 m (3 feet 5 inches)
Total length	7. 16 m (23 feet 6 inches)
Diameter at bottom, above ground level	0. 42 m (16.7 inches)
Diameter at top, below decoration	0. 30 m (11.85 inches)
Diameter of the topmost bulging portion (underground)	0. 48 m (19.09 inches)
Diameter of the base (underground)	0. 62 m (24.59 inches)
Topmost square surface of the decoration	0.304 m x 0.304 m (1 foot x 1 foot)
Diameter of the iron cylinder fitted at the top	0.203 m (8 inches)
Length of the slot for flagstaff	0.152 m (6 inches)
Depth of the flagstaff slot	0.381 m (1 foot 3 inches)

The stone platform around the pillar was built around 1872 and is not an original feature.

Analysis of the dimensions of the pillar (by Balasubramaniam) has revealed its design symmetry. It seems that the original buried base is one-fourth of the total length of the main body of the pillar, excluding the decorative top. The rough surface occupies one-fourth and the smooth surface three-fourths of the main body length of the pillar. This 'analysis of the pillar's relative dimensions' clearly suggests 'that the pillar was originally buried to the start of the smooth surface region'. The rough lower portion of the pillar was thus originally buried and also corroborates the tradition about its being brought from elsewhere and re-erected at its present location.

It has been surmised that the total length of the figure and the decorative capital may have been equal to the same as the portion buried below the ground. This also is a good indicator of the engineering design of the pillar. The Iron Pillar, thus, is not only a superb example of metallurgical engineering and skill but is also important for its historical and astronomical significance.

Qutb Minar

The Qutb Minar (**Fig. VII; Photo 9**), is the most imposing structure in the complex. Originally, the Qutb Minar stood near the south-eastern corner of the Quwwatu'l Islam Masjid. During the second extension of the mosque by Iltutmish in 1229, the Qutb Minar came to be located inside the south-eastern corner of the mosque.

The foundation of the Qutb Minar was laid by Qutbu'd-Din Aibak in 1199. It was perhaps built as a tower of victory as well as a minar attached to the mosque for the muezzin to make the call for prayer. It has been suggested that the minar was 'intended as an outward sign of Islam' and is therefore associated with victory; this is also evident from one of the Nagari inscriptions on the Qutb Minar. That the Qutb Minar was built as a tower of victory is evident from its prototypes at Ghazni (eleventh–twelfth centuries CE), Daulatabad (eleventh century CE), and Siah Posh (tenth century CE) in Afghanistan. The minar at Siah Posh resembles the Qutb Minar in form with its

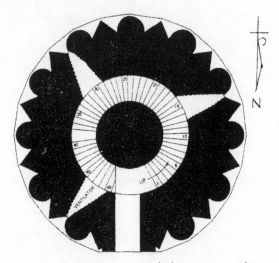

Fig. VII. Qutb Minar, ground plan (not to scale)

alternate semicircular and angular flutings on its exterior face. The minar at Jam was also erected as a tower of victory. Qutbu'd-Din, however, could only raise the first storey of the minar; his son-in-law and successor Iltutmish completed the remaining three storeys. Thus, originally there were only four storeys. The Qutb Minar has at present five storeys: the fifth storey was added along with some changes in the fourteenth century by Firuz Tughluq **(Fig. VIII)**, after it was struck by lightning. In the *Futuhat-i-Firuz Shahi* it is mentioned that the Qutb Minar was not only repaired after it was struck by lightning but also 'raised higher than it was before'. According to the Nagari inscriptions on the minar, it was damaged by lightning twice—in Samvat 1382 (1326 CE) and Samvat 1425 (1369 CE)—during the reign of Muhammad Tughluq and Firuz Tughluq, respectively. Both the inscriptions are engraved in the third balcony of the minar. These Nagari inscriptions are interesting since they mention the exact day and date on which the lightning struck the building; one of these inscriptions also gives the names of the architects who carried out the repairs. Yet another inscription, in Arabic, on the doorway of the fifth storey, mentions the injury caused to the monument by lightning in the year AH 770 (1369 CE) and building of the 'portion of the edifice' by Firuz Shah. We shall return to these inscriptions on the Minar later.

Photo 9. Qutb Minar

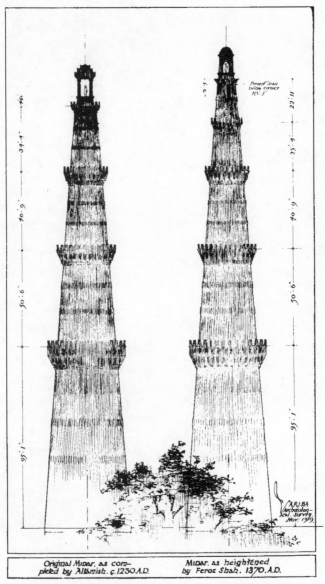

Fig. VIII. Conjectural restoration of the Qutb Minar in silhouette as completed by Iltutmish and as heightened by Firuz Tughluq. From J.A. Page

Rising to the height of 72.5 m (238 feet), the Qutb Minar is the tallest stone tower in India. Its diameter at the base is 14. 40 m (47 feet 3 inches) while on the top it is nearly 2.74 m (9 feet). One has to climb 379 steps to reach its top. (These steps have been repaired in recent years and replaced by new ones with a firm grip so as to allow visitors to go up to the Minar, if and when it is reopened to the public.) The original four storeys had red and buff sandstone veneer; in the course of repairs carried out by Firuz Shah, marble was used in the upper portion of the fourth storey as well as in the fifth, which is completely faced with marble. Originally, there was a cupola atop the Qutb Minar which fell down on 1 August 1803, after an earthquake which also caused other damages to the Minar. Major structural repairs were then carried out between 1805 and 1828. In 1828, the cupola was replaced by a new one built by one Major Smith in the late Mughal style. However, it looked incongruous and was brought down in 1848. It is now placed in the lawns to the south-east of the Minar.

The plan of the Qutb Minar (Fig. VII) is quite ingenuous, varying in each storey. Of the three storeys, the lowest has alternate angular and circular flutings, the second has only round flutings while the third has only angular flutings (Photo 10). The same alignment of flutings is maintained throughout the three storeys, thereby lending a feeling of continuity as well as height. Each storey has a projecting balcony supported by 'stalactite pendentive type of brackets' (Fig. IX) and decorative bands with inscriptions (Photos 10 and 11) which break the monotony and accentuate the effect of the decoration. Most of the inscriptions—in embossed Naskh letters—on each band are quotations from the Quran while some also contain historical information. Thus, the first band, that is, the lowest in the basement storey, mentions 'the Amir, the commander of the army, the glorious, the great', apparently referring to Qutbu'd-Din Aibak.

Inscriptions on the second and fourth bands mention Abul Muzaffar Muhammad ibn Sam, while the third, fifth, and sixth bands carry verses from different Surahs of the Quran. In the second storey are two bands, the lower one mentions 'Abul Muzaffar Iltutmisha-s-Sultani', that is, Shamsu'd-Din Iltutmish, slave of the Sultan Aibak; the upper band has Quranic verses. The doorway of the second storey has the following inscription: 'The completion of this building was commanded

Photo 10. Qutb Minar, first storey balcony showing stalactite ornamentation and Quranic inscriptions

by the king, who is helped from the heavens, (named) Shams-l-Haqwa-d-Din Iltutmisha-l-Qutbi, the helper of the prince of the faithful.'

Of the three inscriptions on the third storey, two mention the name of Iltutmish, one of which is on the doorway; the third, on one side of the door, states: 'This building was completed under the superintendence of the slave, the sinner (named) Muhammad Amir Koh'.

Inscriptions on the fourth storey mention that '(the erection of) this building was ordered during the reign of Shams-ud-Din and was built by Iltutmish'. This inscription, however, is from the time of Firuz Tughluq. This is also recorded in the inscription on the doorway of the fifth storey which states: 'The minar was injured by lightning in (the months of) the year 770 (1369 CE). By the Divine grace Firuz Sultan, who is exalted by the favour of the Most Holy, built this portion of the *muqam* (edifice) with care. May the inscrutable Creator preserve it from all calamities.'

It has been suggested that the Qutb Minar was possibly intended as a tower of victory as well as to serve as a minar attached to the

Fig. IX. Qutb Minar, detail of stalactite corbelling of first storey balcony. From J.A. Page

Photo 11. Qutb Minar, Quranic inscriptions, calligraphy

Quwwatu'l Islam mosque. However, it is more likely that the Minar was 'intended to function as an outward sign of Islam' and could not have served the function of *adhan* (call to prayer). That it was intended as a tower of victory is also evident from three short Nagari inscriptions in the Qutb Minar. A four-line inscription on the left-hand jamb of the fifth slit window in the stairway states: (line 1) *Malikdin ki kiratistambha/*(line 2) *svasti. Bhavatu*(?)/(line 3) *Malakdin/* (line 4) *Malakdin.* The translation is: 'This pillar of fame of Malikdin. May it be for good luck.' The other Nagari inscription on the left-hand abutment of the door of the third balcony reads: (line 1) *Srisulatran Alavadi vi /*(line 2) *jayastambha,* meaning 'The pillar of victory of Sultan Alavadi (i.e., Alau'd-Din)'. The third Nagari inscription is later, being of the year 1332, and reads: (line 1) *Om samat 1389 varshe Chaitrasudi 11 Budha /* (line 2) *dine Srisulatrana Mahmadsahi ki kirati.* It is translated as 'Om. On Wednesday, the 11th of the bright fortnight of Chaitra in the year Samvat 1389 (1332 CE), the [pillar] of fame of the illustrious Sultan Muhammad Shah (Tughluq).'

Though there are quite a few other Nagari inscriptions on the Qutb Minar, most of which provide information, an eight-line inscription in Nagari on the left of the fourth balcony is particularly interesting. It reads:

Line 1. *Om svasti shri suritrana Pherojasha-*
Line 2. *hi vijayaraje(jye) samvat 1426 vari-*
Line 3. *she Phalguna sudi 5 Sukradine mu-*
Line 4. *naro jirnodha (ddha)ra kritam shri Vishva-*
Line 5. *karma pra (pra)sade rachitah sutradhari*
Line 6. *Chahadadevapalasuta (dau)hitra*
Line 7. *sutra [patah nipati-*
Line 8. *ta ude gaja 92]*

The translation is as follows: 'Om. In the auspicious reign of the illustrious Firuz Shah Sultan on Friday the 5th of the bright fortnight of Phalguna in the year Samvat 1426 (1369 CE), the restoration of the Minar was carried out in the palace or temple of Vishvakarma. The architect was the maternal grandson of the son of Chahadadevapala; the measuring cord was drawn and the foundation laid. Height 92 yards.'

Immediately below this inscription is another Nagari inscription which gives dimensions (in yards) of the work done as well as names of two architects Nana and Salha and a carpenter called Dharmu Vanani. Names of Nana and Salha also appear in the Nagari inscription of Samvat 1425 (1328 CE) along with those of two other architects/artisans Lola and Lashman.

Despite the tremors caused by earthquakes and lightning in the last 800 years, the Qutb Minar is standing erect notwithstanding the damage caused to its upper storeys. However, there was a slight tilt in the Minar perhaps even earlier as well which was 'adjusted to some extent as suggested by the offset of the central shaft at the level of reconstruction' by Firuz Shah Tughluq. Investigations about the verticality carried out some years ago also indicated a tilt of 0.635 m (2 feet 1 inch) on the south-west from the perpendicular. Keeping in view the height and diameter of the base, the tilt was however not considered to be serious. The condition of the Qutb Minar is constantly monitored and steps taken to ensure its stability. Studies have been recently done to find ways of improving the seismic resistance of

Qutb Minar. A dynamic monitoring system has been installed in the complex to find clues on quake resistance. After 1828, major structural repairs were carried out during the 1920s, and again from 1944 to 1949. The foundation of the Qutb Minar was also strengthened by grouting in 1971–2, consolidating the loose fabric of masonry and distributing the load of the Minar over a wider area.

'Ala'i Darwaza

To the south-east of the Qutb Minar is the gateway known as the 'Ala'i Darwaza **(Fig. X; Photo 12)**. It was built by 'Alau'd-Din Khalji as the southern entrance to the Quwwatu'l Islam mosque as extended by him. Of the nine inscriptions engraved in different portions of the gate, three inscriptions mention AH 710 (1311 CE) as the date of erection of the mosque for which this gate was built. The name of the builder, 'Alau'd-Din Khalji, is mentioned as Abul Muzaffar Muhammad Shah in as many as nine inscriptions on the 'Ala'i Darwaza. A conspicuous feature of the building is the effective use of inscriptions and geometric designs in the ornamentation of the gateway.

The 'Ala'i Darwaza is regarded as the first building in which the principles of arcuate construction have been employed. Built of red

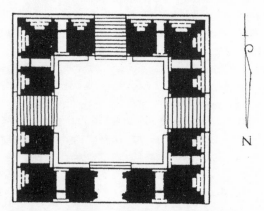

N

Fig. X. 'Ala'i Darwaza, plan (not to scale)

Photo 12. 'Ala'i Darwaza, south and east side gates

sandstone, it is square in plan, and is characterized by a wide and bulging dome with a knob in the centre, pointed horse shoe-shaped and semicircular arches having, what are called, 'lotus-bud' fringes, *jaalis* or perforated screens on the windows framed within horseshoe-shaped arches replicating the ones on the southern entrance doorway. White marble has been used in the inscribed bands and panels that embellish and give a very pleasing look to the building. In fact, the combination of white marble and sandstone breaks the monotony and lends grace to it. The structure is marked by excellent proportions, simplicity, and pierced central openings which accentuate the contour of the dome. The southern gateway of this building with its arabesque decoration clearly suggests Saracenic influence. The 'Ala'i Darwaza is indeed one of the most elegant buildings in the Qutb area.

Tomb of Imam Zamin

Adjacent to the 'Ala'i Darwaza, to its south-east, is the tomb of Imam Muhammad 'Ali, also known as Imam Zamin and Saiyad Hasan Pir Minar **(Photo 13)**. According to the inscription carved on a marble slab over the doorway, the tomb was built in AH 944 (1537–8 CE) in the lifetime of Imam Zamin who died in 1539 CE. Imam Zamin came from Turkestan during the reign of Sikandar Lodi (1488–1517 CE) and is believed to have held some official position connected with the

Photo 13. Tomb of Imam Zamin

Quwwatul' Islam Masjid. The inscription is carved in relief in Naskh characters and states that Muhammad 'Ali was of the Chishtia sect.

It is a small tomb, measuring about 2.23 sq. m (24 square feet) and 16.46 m (54 feet) high from the floor to the top of the pinnacle over the red sandstone dome. On three sides of the tomb are three screens of jaali or lattice-work, while on the southern side is the entrance, which is below the aforementioned inscription. The tomb can be approached through the eastern gateway of the 'Ala'i Darwaza.

Tomb of Iltutmish

To the north-west of the Quwwatul' Islam mosque, just behind the corner of the extension carried out by Shamsu'd-Din Iltutmish (1211–36 CE) lies his tomb **(Fig. XI)**. Iltutmish was the son-in-law and successor of Qutbu'd-Din Aibak. The tomb was built by Iltutmish himself in about 1235, a year before his death. Curiously enough, there is no inscription in the tomb ascribing it to Iltutmish.

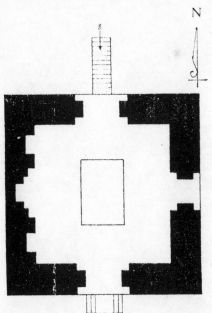

Fig. XI. Tomb of Iltutmish, plan (not to scale)

The tomb is square on plan, each side being 9 m (29 feet 6 inches) internally and is plain on the exterior while its interior is profusely ornamented **(Photo 14)**. The existing building is domeless, however, there may have existed a dome originally as is evident from the squinch arch at the corners of the building. It may be mentioned that the squinch arch as a device to build a dome was used for the first time in this building. It is also interesting to mention that the squinches were laid in this building by corbelling which was the indigenous method. Firuz Shah Tughluq is said to have replaced the dome after the original fell down. This too did not survive. The cenotaph is in the centre of the tomb, while the grave is in the crypt or the mortuary chamber below, entry into which is from the north. The cenotaph is mainly of marble, resting on a base measuring 4.26 m (14 feet) by 2.74 m (9 feet) and is 2.31 m (7 feet 7 inches) high **(Photo 14)**.

Photo 14. Iltutmish's tomb, interior

Entrance into the mausoleum is from three sides while on the west wall are three mihrabs for offering prayers. The central mihrab is higher than the other two with profusely carved decoration and distinct because of the use of marble. The ornamentation is mainly in the form of beautifully carved Quranic inscriptions, arabesque and floral motifs and designs framing the arched mihrab **(Photo 15).** The inscriptions are in Kufic as well as Naskh and are either embossed or in high relief. In fact, the entire interior surface of the tomb is profusely decorated in this manner and is an important feature of this tomb. One can also notice typical Hindu motifs like the wheel, chain-and-bell, lotus, and diamond as well. The entrance doorways—4.87 m (16 feet) high, set within shallow arched recesses about 8.23 m (27 feet) high—to the tomb have also been elaborately decorated with Quranic texts and geometric patterns. An eminent authority on Indian architecture, James Fergusson, called the tomb 'one of the richest examples of Hindu art applied to Muhammadan purposes that old Delhi affords, and is extremely beautiful'.

'Alau'd-Din's Madrasa

'Alau'd-Din's madrasa **(Fig. XII)** is to the south-west of the Quwwatu'l Islam Masjid. It was established by 'Alau'd-Din Khalji (1296–1316 CE) to impart education in Islamic theology and scriptures. It comprises of rooms and halls built around a quadrangular court, entry into which was from the north side through an impressive triple gateway, the central one being the biggest.

'Alau'd-Din's Tomb

The large square structure located on the south side of the court of the madrasa is believed to be the tomb of Sultan 'Alau'd-Din Khalji **(Fig. XII; Photo 16).** It was originally covered by a dome and a boldly projecting portico, both of which have now fallen. The western wall of the tomb has a small niche meant for offering prayers.

Photo 15. Iltutmish's tomb, central mihrab with inscriptions in Kufic and Naskh characters

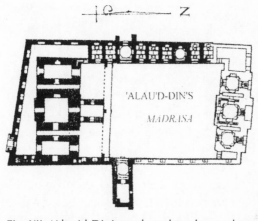

Fig. XII. 'Alau'd-Din's tomb and madrasa, plan
(not to scale)

Photo 16. 'Alau'd-Din's tomb

'Ala'i Minar

This unfinished minar **(Fig. XIII; Photo 17)** was envisaged by its builder 'Alau'd-Din Khalji as a part of his grandiose scheme to enlarge the Quwwatu'l Islam Masjid to twice its size. The 'Ala'i Minar was accordingly planned also to be double the size of the Qutb Minar, keeping in view the proportions of the enlarged Quwwatu'l Islam Masjid. Due to the death of 'Alau'd-Din, both enlargements remained incomplete. The probable date of the construction of this Minar is c. 1315 CE.

The 'Ala'i Minar can be seen to the north of the Quwwatu'l Islam Masjid standing over a high platform or base unlike the Qutb Minar which has no platform. This square platform of the minar was exposed by ASI in the course of excavations in the year 1912. Of its several distinctive features, prominent are the angular flutings on the exterior, a ramp inside with a gentle slope from right to left for ascending and an entrance doorway towards the east. A visit to the minar can help in understanding the technique of the construction of the Qutb Minar.

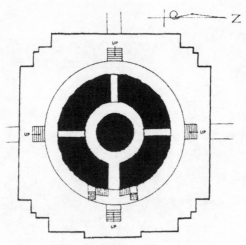

Fig. XIII. 'Ala'i Minar, plan (not to scale)

Photo 17. 'Ala'i Minar

Other Monuments within the Qutb Complex

On the lawns of the Qutb complex is kept the red sandstone *chhatri* or canopy which was placed atop the Qutb Minar in 1828 after the chhatri erected by Firuz Tughluq fell down. It was removed in 1848 since it was found to be architecturally incongruous with the Minar. Close to the western gateway of the late Mughal sarai is a small mosque having a vaulted roof and three-arched entrance.

THREE

Monuments to the South and South-east of the Qutb Complex

I n the area contiguous to the Qutb complex, there are some
monuments towards the south and south-east and on both sides
of the road to Gurgaon. Prominent among these are: the walls
of Lal Kot and Chaumukha Darwaza, Dilkusha comprising the tomb
of Quli Khan and other remains, Jamali Kamali mosque and tomb,
Madhi Masjid, and Balban's tomb. This area forms part of the Mehrauli
Archaeological Park.

Lal Kot and Chaumukha Darwaza

While the remains of Lal Kot are better preserved to the north of
the Qutb complex, behind the Yogamaya temple, one can still see
traces of the walls and small semi-circular bastions of Lal Kot to the
south-east of the Qutb complex adjoining the Chaumukha Darwaza.
The Chaumukha Darwaza, meaning gate with four openings **(Photo
18)**, however, is a later building, and can be dated perhaps to the
Tughluq period (1320–1414 CE).

Photo 18. Chaumukha Darwaza

Dilkusha

Sir Charles Theophilus Metcalfe, British Resident at the Mughal court, built this pleasure garden in the early nineteenth century. Dilkusha is located about 150 m (490 feet) to the south-east of the Qutb Minar. It was planned as a formal garden, with a central pavilion, terraces, and watercourses, besides an early seventeenth-century tomb which Metcalfe modified to fit into his scheme. The tomb, octagonal in shape and standing on a high platform, was of Muhammad Quli Khan, brother of Adham Khan (who was a general and foster-brother of Akbar). Metcalfe extended the tomb on all sides, creating chambers around the central dining space which was in the main tomb itself. These structures were erected in what is called the pseudo-Mughal style and are known as Metcalfe's follies. Some of these are extant like the two pyramidal towers, called Garhgaj.

It is said that Metcalfe had bought the tomb to save it from demolition and develop the landscape and create a garden. According to Sayyid Ahmed Khan, Metcalfe Kothi Dilkusha was built in AH 1260 (1844 CE). This resort, which was used by Metcalfe mainly during the rains, can be reached through a gate in the northern enclosure wall of the garden.

Jamali Kamali's Mosque and Tomb

About 457 m (1500 feet) to the south of Muhammad Quli Khan's tomb are located the mosque of Jamali Kamali and the tomb of Maulana Jamali **(Fig. XIV; Photo 19)**. Jamali was the pen name of Shaikh Fazlu'llah alias Jalal Khan. A contemporary of Babur and Humayun, he composed poems eulogizing them. After his death in Gujarat in AH 942 (1535–6 CE), where he had accompanied Humayun, his body was brought to Delhi and buried in this tomb which he had built for himself in AH 935 (1528–9 CE) during the reign of Babur.

The tomb is located within an enclosure, the walls of which are battlemented and provided with panels containing niches. The tomb proper is square on plan with a flat roof. The structure is built of stone rubble and embellished with a band of blue tiles beneath the chhajja and blue and green tiles in the parapet on the exterior, while

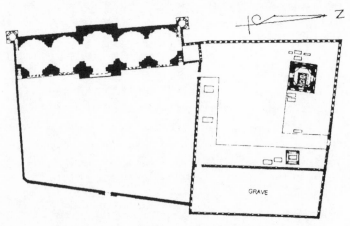

Fig. XIV. Jamali Kamali's mosque and tomb, plan (not to scale)

Photo 19. Jamali Kamali's mosque, view of five arched openings and dome above the central arch opening

the interior is elaborately ornamented with tiles as well as incised and painted plaster. Under the ceiling are incised, in plaster, verses composed by Maulana Jamali himself. At the centre of the tomb is Jamali's grave. There is another grave to its east which is said to be that of Kamali; hence the name Jamali Kamali given to the tomb. However, it is not possible to confirm this name.

The mosque of Jamali-Kamali is to the south of the tomb. Erected in about AH 935 (1528–9 CE), it is an elegant building, rectangular in plan with five bays and a large forecourt. On the west wall of the mosque are five recessed mihrabs at the end of each bay; the central and northern mihrabs are decorated with Quranic inscriptions. Except for the ceiling of the central compartment, which is octagonal formed by elegant pendentives, the rest are flat. The mosque is surmounted by a high dome in the centre. Over the central opening of the mosque is a small balcony window around which is an elaborately carved frame supported on either side by a fluted pilaster of red sandstone with carved bands. On the back wall of the mosque are three windows with bracketed balconies. Use of red and grey sandstone as well as marble is a feature of this mosque.

The mosque is an interesting example of Lodi style as is evident from some of the features that are borrowed from its prototype, the Moth Masjid (also called Moth ki Masjid) near South Extension, New Delhi, which was built by Miyan Bhuwa, a minister of Sikandar Lodi (1488–1517 CE). Some of the features of the Jamali Kamali mosque can also be seen in the Qal'a-i-Kuhna Masjid built inside the Purana Qila in 1541 CE. The Jamali Kamali mosque therefore occupies an important position in the evolution of mosque design in India.

Balban's Tomb

At a distance of about 275 m (900 feet) from the Jamali Kamali tomb and mosque is located a highly dilapidated rubble-built structure **(Photo 20)**. It is now without a dome. Square on plan with arched openings on all four sides, it occupies an important place in the development of Indo-Islamic architecture since a true arch was used for the first

Photo 20. Balban's tomb

time in this building. This building is believed to be the tomb of
Ghiyathu'd-Din Balban (1265–87 CE).

Madhi Masjid

About half a kilometre south of the Jamali-Kamali Masjid is a mosque
popularly known as Madhi Masjid **(Fig. XV; Photo 21)**. It combines
the features of an open-wall mosque and a covered mosque which
makes it unusual. The three central bays on the wall-mosque have
flat-roofed chambers with arched openings. The gateway on the
eastern side is domed and looks very impressive. The mosque is
decorated with a profusion of ornamental tiles. The mosque is either
of the Lodi or early Mughal period.

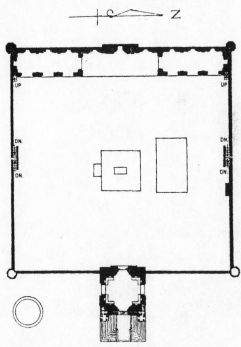

Fig. XV. Madhi Masjid, plan (not to scale)

Photo 21. Madhi Masjid

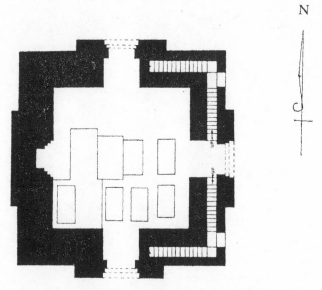

N

Fig. XVI. Tomb of Azim Khan, plan (not to scale)

Tomb of Azim Khan

On the eastern side of the road to Gurgaon is a tomb on a prominent rock which is said to be that of Akbar Khan or Azim Khan (**Fig. XVI**). Built sometime in the early seventeenth century, it is a plain square domed structure coated with plaster and decorated with incised work. Its doorways are of red sandstone. The gravestone is missing. Close by, on the same rock is a gateway of stone believed to have been built by Metcalfe.

FOUR

Monuments in and around Mehrauli

There are a number of other monuments in Mehrauli and in the close vicinity of the Qutb complex towards the north and north-east. These belong to different periods, ranging from the vestiges of Lal Kot and its subsequent enlargement which goes by the name of Qila Rai Pithora, Anang Tal, to other buildings of later periods, for example, Adham Khan's tomb, Yogamaya temple, baolis or step-wells, tanks and gardens, sarais, mosques, tombs and graves, a palace, dargah, havelis or mansions, and even a *kabutar khana* or pigeon house. In fact, monuments are scattered all over the area where one could go for a ramble.

Lal Kot and Qila Rai Pithora

Not much remains of Lal Kot, the Tomar citadel built by Anangpal (*c.* 1050–60 CE), except for the vestiges which are traceable only at places **(Figs II and III)**. The remains can be seen to the north-west of the Qutb complex, close to Adham Khan's tomb, behind the Yogamaya temple and to some extent to the south-east of the Qutb near the Chaumukha gate. Construction of roads and other building activity have largely destroyed Lal Kot save for remnants that can only be seen few and far between.

The citadel was originally oblong on plan, with its thick stone-built ramparts pierced by gates. The walls, about 2.3–3 m ($7\frac{1}{2}$–10 feet) thick, were built of random rubble over a stone footing above which was a thick brick revetment. Outside the rampart was a moat of which only some traces can now be seen. The area of Lal Kot was enlarged sometime in the thirteenth century when several semicircular bastions and gates were provided which are known as the Ranjit or Ghazni gate, Fateh gate, and Sohan gate. The biggest bastion was towards the north-west and is known as the Sohan Burj (Fig. III).

The temples which were destroyed to provide material for the construction of the Quwwatu'l Islam Masjid, as recorded in the inscription on the eastern entrance gateway of the mosque, may have been located inside Lal Kot. This is also evident from the high platform over which the original mosque was built.

Some portions of Lal Kot have been exposed by the ASI in the course of excavations from time to time. Remains of the Anang Tal, which was located inside Lal Kot and buried under accumulated debris, have also been exposed. This tank was filled by harvesting water from the surrounding catchment area. The Anang Tal was roughly oblong on plan in view of the contours and physical features of the area; during the course of his survey of the area in 1862–3, Alexander Cunningham had measured the dimensions of the tank as 51.51 x 46.33 x 12.19 m (169 feet north-south x 152 feet east-west x 40 feet depth). At the time of Cunningham's visit, the tank was dry and filled with debris; it is however recorded that water was used from the Anang Tal by 'Alau'd-Din Khalji during the construction of the 'Ala'i Minar. As a result of archaeological excavations, steps have been partially exposed on the north-east corner and southern side of the Anang Tal (Fig. XVII). An interesting feature was pairs of steps arranged in pyramidal fashion on the northern and eastern sides at different levels. This not only made access into the reservoir easier but also broke the monotony of the structure. In fact, there are several contemporary and even earlier tanks which have similar features; the tank in front of the Sun temple at Modhera in Gujarat is a beautiful example of this type of construction. Presence of masons'

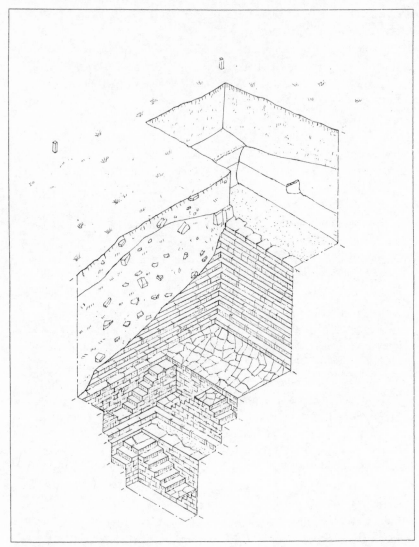

Fig. XVII. Lal Kot: 1994–5. Partly exposed north-eastern corner of Anang
Tal. After B.R. Mani

marks on some of the stones has provided evidence of the construction
of the tank sometime in the middle of the eleventh century.

During the course of excavations, remains of the structures of
the Sultanate period including a palace complex **(Fig. XVIII)**
comprising rooms, water cisterns, etc., were exposed along with
different kinds of antiquities and typical pottery.

Delhi was captured from the Tomars by King Vigraharaja IV
(*c.* 1153–64 CE) (also known as Bisaldeo) of the Chahamana or
Chauhan dynasty. His nephew Prithviraja III popularly known as
Rai Pithora, extended Lal Kot to its north, east and south, thereby
enlarging it. The massive ramparts of the citadel, about 9.14 m (30
feet) in thickness and about 18.28 m (60 feet) in height with a moat
all around, have been pierced at places by roads in recent times **(Fig.
II)**. The Qila was captured by Qutbu'd-Din Aibak in 1192 who made
the fort his capital. Qila Rai Pithora finds mention in several accounts
of the Sultanate period. According to Timur, the fort had ten gates;
of these the Hauz Rani, Barka, and Budaun gates still exist. The poet
Amir Khusrau (1253–1325 CE), in his description of Delhi, says that
it had thirteen gates. The Moorish traveller Ibn Battuta, who was in
India from 1333 to 1346 during the reign of Muhammad bin Tughluq
(1325–51 CE), mentions in his account the Budaun gate which was
perhaps the main entrance to the city. The walls of Qila Rai Pithora
were repaired earlier by 'Alau'd-Din Khalji (1296–1316 CE) and also
by Qutbu'd-Din Mubarak Shah (1316–20 CE).

Remains of the Qila Rai Pithora have been excavated and
conserved by ASI.

Adham Khan's Tomb

The tomb of Adham Khan **(Fig. XIX; Photo 22)** is located to the
north-west of the Qutb complex, on the road to Mehrauli. Locally called
the *Bhulbhulaiyan*, meaning labyrinth, it is situated in a commanding
position, having been built over the walls of Lal Kot and on a high
platform or terrace enclosed by an octagonal wall with low towers at
the corners. The tomb proper is octagonal, with a verandah on each
side, surmounted by a dome. Each verandah has three arches.

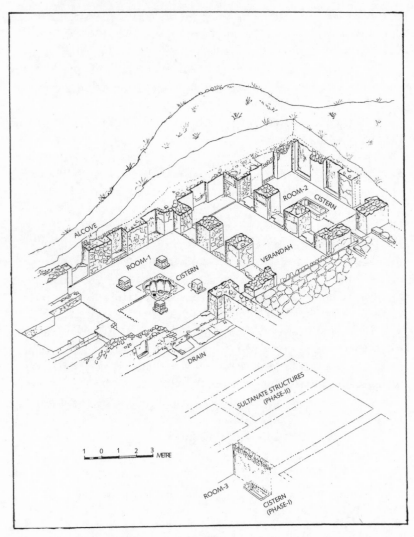

Fig. XVIII. Lal Kot: 1992–4. View of partly exposed early Sultanate palace complex. After B.R. Mani

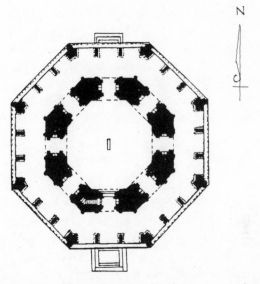

Fig. XIX. Adham Khan's tomb, plan (not to scale)

Photo 22. Adham Khan's tomb

Adham Khan was a nobleman holding the rank of 5000 and a general in Akbar's army. In 1562, he killed Shamsu'd-Din Ataga Khan, foster-father of Akbar and the husband of Ji Ji Anga (also known as Maham Angah) his foster-mother. The emperor Akbar (1556–1605 CE) ordered that he should be thrown to his death from the ramparts of the Agra Fort. His mother Maham Angah died of grief soon after and is buried with her son in this tomb built by Akbar.

Yogamaya Temple

The Yogamaya or Jogamaya temple is located to the south of the Anang Tal, about 92 m (300 feet) to the north-west of the Qutb enclosure. According to tradition, the temple has a hoary antiquity as is evident from Yoginipura, one of the ancient names of Delhi. The present temple was built in the Later Mughal period during the reign of Akbar II (1806–37) and has been renovated and added to in recent years. The shrine is frequented by the devout particularly during Navaratri. During the Phoolwalon ki Sair, held in early October, fans made of flowers are presented at the shrine.

Zafar Mahal Complex

Located outside the Ajmeri gate or the Naya Darwaza which is the western entrance of the Dargah Qutb Sahib, this palace complex **(Fig. XX; Photo 23)** was built by the Akbar II (1806–37). The main entrance gateway of the palace was rebuilt by the last Mughal emperor, Bahadur Shah II (1837–57). The three-storeyed gateway built of red sandstone is said to have been rebuilt to allow elephants to enter. The gateway has a broad chhajja and small projecting windows covered with curved 'Bengali' domes. Inside the gate is a spacious arcade with arched compartments on either side. A wide stairway leads to the rooms on the upper floor. In the south-western corner of Zafar Mahal is the Rang Mahal built by Bahadur Shah II. On the eastern side are the *dalans* of the time of Jahandar Shah.

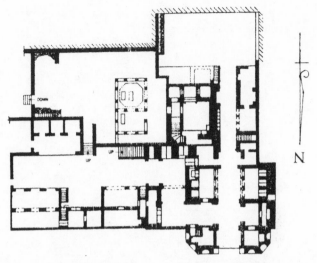

Fig. XX. Zafar Mahal complex, plan (not to scale)

Photo 23. Zafar Mahal complex

Contiguous to the Zafar Mahal are some old havelis and other old buildings of Late Mughal times.

Dargah Qutb Sahib

The dargah **(Photo 24)** occupies an important place in Mehrauli. It contains the mortal remains of Khwaja Qutbu'd-Din Bakhtyar Kaki who came from a place called Ush in Persia. He became a disciple of Khwaja Mu'inu'd-Din Chishti of Ajmer whom he succeeded as a spiritual preceptor. He lived during the reign of Iltutmish (1211–36) and died in 1236.

The main shrine of the dargah is a domed rectangular enclosure embellished by multicoloured tiles. It contains the grave of Qutb Sahib who was held in high esteem particularly by different rulers who are also buried in the different enclosures around the main shrine. Of the several graves, noteworthy are those of Bahadur Shah I (1707–12), Shah Alam II (1759–1806), Akbar II (1806–37) and their

Photo 24. Dargah Qutb Sahib

family members, the nawabs of Jhajjhar, Loharu, Banda, and several others. Bahadur Shah II had also prepared a grave for his burial here but it remained unutilized.

There are mosques, gates and other buildings in the dargah erected in different periods. Among the prominent ones are the Moti Masjid (meaning 'pearl mosque') **(Fig. XXI; Photo 25)**, Naubat

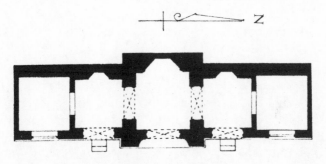

Fig. XXI. Moti Masjid, plan (not to scale)

Photo 25. Moti Masjid

Khana or the drum house, Majlis Khana (assembly house), and Tosh
Khana (robe chamber). There are also tanks and a baoli or step-well
which measures 29.26 m (96 feet) x 12.8 m (42 feet) and is 22.86 m
(75 feet) deep. This baoli was built in 1846.

During the Sair-i-Gulfaroshan or the Phoolwalon ki Sair, flower
fans are presented at the dargah.

Jahaz Mahal

The Jahaz Mahal **(Fig. XXII; Photo 26)** is located at the south-
east corner of the Hauz-i-Shamsi. Built sometime during the Lodi
period (1451–1526), it may have been used either as a pleasure
resort or as accommodation for pilgrims. It contains a courtyard,
several chambers, square chhatris at the corners, and a gateway
surmounted by a domed pavilion which is embellished with blue
tiles. It is called Jahaz Mahal perhaps because of its appearance as
a *jahaz* or ship.

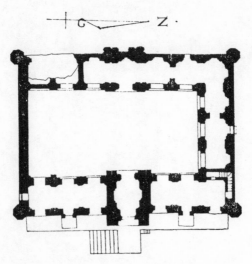

Fig. XXII. Jahaz Mahal, plan (not to scale)

Photo 26. Jahaz Mahal

Hauz-i-Shamsi

Located on the southern outskirts of Mehrauli, this tank **(Fig. XXIII)** was built in AH 627 (1229–30 CE) by Shamsu'd-Din Iltutmish (1211–36 CE) and derives its name after him. The waters of the tank are considered sacred because of an interesting story about the foundation of the tank. According to tradition, Prophet Muhammad once appeared in a dream riding a horse and pointed out the site to Iltutmish to build the tank. The following morning, the king went in the company of Qutb Sahib to the place pointed out by the Prophet where he found a hoof mark of the Prophet's horse. He noticed that water was oozing out from the spot. He built a tank there as well as a platform and a dome over the hoof-print. The tank was cleared by 'Alau'd-Din Khalji in AH 711 (1311–12 CE) and repaired by Firuz Tughluq. Firuz Tughluq, in his *Futuhat-i-Firuz Shahi*, mentions that the Hauz-i-Shamsi or the tank of

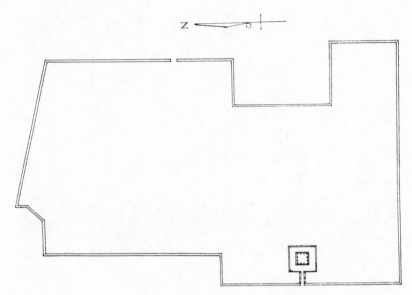

Fig. XXIII. Hauz-i-Shamsi, plan (not to scale)

Iltutmish, 'had been deprived of water by some graceless men, who stopped up the channels of supply. I punished these incorrigible men severely, and opened again the closed up channels'. The Moorish traveller Ibn-Battuta was struck by the size of the tank which is said to have originally covered more than 40.46 hectares or 100 acres (276 bighas).

Jharna

This block of buildings is called Jharna **(Photo 27)**, meaning waterfall, which drains off the surplus water from the Hauz-i-Shamsi. Nawab Ghaziu'd-Din Khan Firuz Jang built the colonnaded dalan containing the waterfall in about 1700. Akbar II (1806–37) constructed the pavilions to the north while Bahadur Shah II (1837–57) added a *baradari* in the centre between the two tanks.

Photo 27. Jharna

Rajon ki Bain

Rajon ki Bain is a baoli or step-well **(Fig. XXIV; Photo 28)**, deriving its name from the word *raj* meaning mason, perhaps because it was used for a time by masons. It forms a complex along with a mosque and a chhatri, all belonging to the Lodi period (1451–1526 CE).

The step-well is oblong, oriented north-south, with steps leading to the well at the southern end. It has four storeys, the lowest of which is decorated with small, deeply recessed arches. The topmost level of the step-well as well as the second storey has an arcade with massive piers. Steps on its top wall connect it with the mosque which is on a higher level. The mosque consists of three compartments each entered through a doorway under two recessed arches. In the west wall is the mihrab recess; the central mihrab is decorated with Quranic inscriptions cut in plaster. In the courtyard of the mosque is a chhatri crowned by a dome which springs from a sixteen-sided drum inlaid with blue tiles.

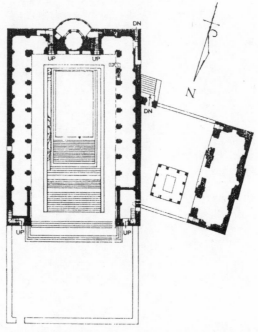

Fig. XXIV. Rajon ki Bain, plan (not to scale)

Photo 28. Rajon ki Bain

Above the chhajja is a frieze of grey stone and plaster inlaid with blue tiles. Inside the chhatri is a grave. Above the chhajja on the south side is an inscription on a red sandstone slab dated AH 918 (1512 CE) of the time of Sikandar Shah (1489–1517 CE), son of Bahlul Shah.

Gandhak ki Baoli

This baoli or stepwell **(Fig. XXV; Photo 29)** is also known as the diving-well because of persons diving from its top into the well.

The name Gandhak ki Baoli connotes the presence of sulphur in the water which is believed to possess healing properties. The baoli is located close to the Dargah Qutb Sahib and is about 92 m (300 feet) to the south of Adham Khan's tomb.

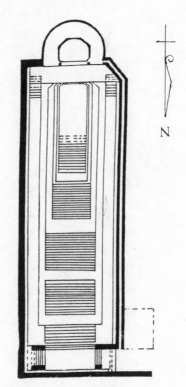

N

The baoli is oriented north-south and measures 40.5 m (133 feet) in length and 10.6 m (34 feet 9 inches) in width. The baoli is in five tiers, each tier narrowing as it descends towards the bottom. The circular well is at the southern end of the baoli and can be reached by the flight of steps. Each tier is reached by way of galleries on the east and west which give access to the circular portion of the well. The top gallery of the well has a range of columns. Built of coarse rubble of uniform size, the baoli dates back to the reign of Iltutmish (1210–35 CE).

Fig. XXV. Gandhak ki Baoli, plan (not to scale)

Photo 29. Gandhak ki Baoli

Practical Tips and Information

The best time to visit Delhi is between September/October and March. From late March Delhi starts getting warm with temperature ranging between 24° C and 40° C (75.2° F and 104° F) even rising sometime up to about 46° C (115° F) in June. Monsoon arrives towards the end of June or early July and lasts till September. Delhi being in the rain shadow zone, intensity of rainfall is less and not consistent, the average being about 500 mm (19.68 inches) during monsoon. Rains are enjoyable, although it may get oppressively sultry sometimes. October onwards Delhi weather becomes pleasant and enjoyable. It gets cold in December–January when the day temperature may be around 18° C (64° F) and could go down to 4° C (39° F) or even lower in the night.

Apart from the large number of monuments, which attract visitors to this city, Delhi is at its resplendent best in the months of February–March with flowers of different hues and fragrance blooming everywhere, justifying the sobriquet of garden city. The well-manicured lawns and gardens around the monuments enhance the ambience. In the Qutb complex there are trees like *Salvadora persica* or *Salvadora oloeides* (Hindi, *pilu* or *dungar*), *Ficus lyrata* (which is of African origin) with its large leaves, *Azadirachta indica* (neem), *Terminalia arjuna* (*arjun*), *Tamarindus indica* (tamarind or *imli*), *Cycas revoluta* (sago cycad), and other plants, shrubs and seasonal flowers. The rocky landscape, forming part of the Aravallis with its *Acacia nilotica* (*kikar* or *babool*) and *Capparis aphylla* (*karil*) trees and the bright scarlet flowers of *Butea monosperma* or *Butea frondosa* (*dhak* or *palash*), the sweet and delectable *Zizyphus mauritania* (*ber*), different scrubs, other thorny bushes and plants have their own attraction. The majestic *Ficus religiosa* (*pipal*) and other *Ficus* trees, besides neem, *arjun*, *Eugenia jambolana* (*jamun*), *Salmalia malabarica* (*semal*), *Cassia fistula* (*amaltas*), *Delonix regia* (*gulmohar*), etc., are some of the other plants which add colour to Delhi's landscape. The variety of indigenous trees and plants, in the New Delhi area, the Lodi Gardens, and other monuments will fascinate any visitor to Delhi.

Monuments

Barring a few monuments, entry into most monuments will cost Rs 5 for Indians and Rs 100 or $2 for foreigners. For Qutb and Humayun's Tomb, which are World Heritage monuments, entry fee is Rs 10 for Indians and Rs 250 or $5 for foreigners. Entry for children below 15 years of age is free. One can take still photographs of the monuments without paying any fee; for using a video camera, an amount of Rs 25 is charged. One can also enjoy the sound and light show at the Red Fort, except during monsoons when it is temporarily suspended. The Qutb complex is also now floodlit and visitors are allowed entry into selected areas up to 10.00 p.m.

Reaching Delhi

Air: Delhi is connected with practically all the major cities and towns of India. All major airlines operate from Delhi, some of them having multiple flights to and from Delhi. Delhi Airport is called Indira Gandhi International Airport (IGIA) and has two terminals, Terminal 1 for domestic flights and Terminal 2 for international flights. The distance between the two terminals is about 7 km.

Most international airlines connect Delhi with the rest of the world. Offices of the major international airlines are mainly located in and around Connaught Place (officially Rajiv Chowk) which is about 19 km from Terminal 2 and 12 km from Terminal 1 of the airport.

Travelling by air to Delhi is convenient though fog may sometimes delay flights during winter.

Visitors should preferably hire the pre-paid taxis available from both the domestic and international terminals. Air-conditioned taxis, dial-a-cab, white taxis with registration no. starting with DLY as well as black taxis with yellow-top can be hired from these airports. Buses of Delhi Transport Undertaking and Ex-Servicemen's Transport also operate with fixed point-to-point rates between the airport and Connaught Place. Three-wheeler autos are also available outside the domestic terminal; most of them avoid using the fare meter which can be inconvenient.

Rail: Indian Railways has a vast network of inter-city and long-distance trains connecting Delhi from its five railway stations respectively at Old Delhi, New Delhi, Nizamuddin, Sarai Rohilla, and Delhi Cantonment. Superfast Rajdhani trains connect Delhi with major metropolitan cities and state capitals; Shatabdi and Jan Shatabdi trains connect the important towns. These are chair-car trains.

It is advisable to book tickets in advance particularly in the summer months when schools and other educational institutions close for vacations as well as in October–November which is the season of several fairs and festivals.

General information on Indian Railways, including train schedules can be obtained on the internet by logging on to *www.indianrail.gov.in*. Online ticket booking can be done by logging on to *www. irctc.co.in*. Advance booking for tickets can be done across the counter at the railway stations and railway booking offices in different localities of Delhi.

Accommodation at reasonable rates is provided at the Rail Yatri Niwas in New Delhi, where independent rooms, with or without A/C and dormitories can be booked on the production of rail ticket.

Special tourist trains, like the Palace on Wheels, and the Fairy Queen, with a fixed itinerary, are also available from Delhi.

Indian Railways also offers concessions to senior citizens, orthopaedically handicapped, and others afflicted by blindness, cancer, thalassaemia, etc.

It is always advisable to travel from the railway station by taking pre-paid taxi or three-wheeler scooter. Where this facility is not available, these should be hired from the authorized stand and payment should be made according to the meter.

It would be worthwhile buying the latest edition of *Trains at a Glance* published every July by the Indian Railways for more information. It is useful and inexpensive.

Bus and other modes of public transport: Delhi does not have a very efficient public transport system. The Delhi Transport Undertaking, which is a shade better but deficient in periodicity, and private buses called blue lines (pejoratively referred to as 'killer buses'), are used for commuting by the general public. For Qutb Minar, buses ply from the Old Delhi, New Delhi, and Nizamuddin railway stations as well as from some of the Inter-State Bus Terminals (ISBTs) from where long-distance buses to places outside Delhi are also available. Rajasthan Tourism Development Corporation also operates regular bus services to different towns in Rajasthan from Bikaner House (India Gate).

The Delhi Transport Undertaking and Delhi Tourism also organize regular conducted city tours of different duration. A visit to the Qutb Minar is almost always included in these tours.

Metro Rail: With the introduction of the Metro Rail in Delhi, commuting has become easier for thousands of people travelling long distances in the city. The Metro Rail has not been extended to south Delhi as yet; but in a few years it may perhaps be possible to take a Metro to the Qutb.

Tourist Offices and State Information Centres

Tourists should avoid touts and the so-called tourist information centres near the railway stations and the airport managed by private persons. The Tourism Department of the Government of India has a Tourist Office at 88 Janpath (Connaught Place) and the Delhi Tourism and Transportation Development Corporation has a chain of offices at many locations in Delhi with the central office in the Bombay Life Building, N Block, Middle Circle, Connaught Place. Services of reputed travel agents could be availed for planning visits.

Information centres of most states are on Baba Kharak Singh Marg, near Connaught Place, where there are also state emporias offering a variety of handicrafts and other products typical of that state. A few states have their information centres in Chanakyapuri where most embassies and high commissions are located.

Shopping

Besides the state emporia on Baba Kharak Singh Marg, the visitor to Delhi can also shop at Dilli Haat, not very far from the Qutb, where craftspersons from different parts of India sell their wares. The Crafts Museum, near Purana Qila, also offers craft demonstrations and sale of material produced by craftspersons. Shopping at the government-owned Central Cottage Industries Emporium at Janpath is also worthwhile.

Shopping in Delhi is a great experience. There are so many places one could go to for shopping. Practically all localities have shopping centres and markets besides shopping malls in some areas. Connaught Place in New Delhi or Chandni Chowk in Old Delhi, Ajmal Khan Road in Karol Bagh, and Central Market in Lajpat Nagar are among the more popular places for shopping. A visit to Sarojini Nagar or Janpath's pavement shops to buy inexpensive garments can be an interesting experience.

Note: Visitors should avoid buying antiques since permission is invariably not given for export of antiquities and certain modern works of art which have been declared as art treasures.

Museums and Picture Galleries

The National Museum, located on Janpath, showcases a range of Indian sculpture, bronzes, paintings, coins, jewellery, archaeological artefacts, manuscripts, textiles, anthropological material besides the archaeological material collected from Central Asia by Sir Aurel Stein. In the Red Fort, the ASI is maintaining three museums: Archaeological Museum housed in the Mumtaz Mahal, containing material mostly belonging to the Mughal period; Indian War Memorial Museum housed in the upper storey of the Naubat- or Naqqar-khana displays mainly arms and armour and other war memorabilia; and the Swatantrata Sangram Sangrahalaya, in one of the barracks of the British period, showcasing India's freedom struggle. ASI has also set up an Archaeological Museum at the Purana Qila where excavated material has been displayed along with photographs of the archaeological remains unearthed at this site.

Close to Rajghat, the samadhi of Mahatma Gandhi, is the Gandhi Memorial Museum. *Eternal Gandhi*, a multimedia presentation on Mahatma Gandhi can be experienced at 5, Tees January Marg in New Delhi.

The National Rail Museum, National Gallery of Modern Art, Crafts Museum, and the Nehru Memorial Museum and Library are also worth a visit.

All museums of Red Fort remain closed on Mondays and the one at Purana Qila on Fridays.

Accommodation

Visitors to Delhi have a wide range of choice for accommodation, from swanky five-star hotels to tourist lodges for those on a budget. Most of the budget tourist lodges are in Connaught Place, Karol Bagh, Paharganj, and Chandni Chowk while there are also private lodging houses in several localities and near the railway stations and the airport. The YMCA Tourist Hostel, YWCA International Guest House, and the International Youth Hostel are some other inexpensive places where one could stay. While accommodation to suit all kinds of visitors is available almost all over Delhi, it is always advisable to plan and make advance reservations, particularly in winter when the tourist season is at its peak.

Glossary

adhan (pronounced *azaan*)	:	Muslim call to prayer by the *muezzin*
Adinatha	:	first Jaina Tirthankara. Also known as Rishabhanatha or Rishabhadeva
arabesque decoration	:	a type of decoration based on flowers, leaves, and branches which are often intertwined, found especially in Islamic art
Ashoka	:	Maurya emperor who is dated *c.* 273–236 BCE
Ashokan pillar	:	highly polished stone pillars (mostly sandstone) which Ashoka got erected in different parts of his kingdom. These pillars had a capital on top, which varied from site to site. The pillars contained edicts issued by Emperor Ashoka, engraved on the pillars. The emblem of the Government of India comprising three lions is taken from the Ashokan pillar capital at Sarnath which has four lions *dos-a-dos* (back to back).
baoli	:	step-well. These are very typical structures, usually oblong, with steps, landings and sometime galleries, leading to a circular well at the other end.

baradari	:	pillared pavilion with twelve openings (*dar*), hence the nomenclature
BCE	:	Before Common Era or Before Christian Era
'Bengali' dome	:	curved dome; roof with a curvature shaped like the curved roof of a hut
bhulbhulaiyan	:	labyrinth, maze
Bisaldeo	:	popular name of Chahamana king Vigraharaja IV (*c*. 1153–64 CE), king of Shakambhari, modern Sambhar in Rajasthan, son of Analladeva; also known as Visaldeo, Visaladeva
CE	:	Common Era, equivalent to AD
Chahamana	:	dynasty which captured Delhi from the Tomars sometime in the twelfth century. Also known by the name of Chauhans
chain-and-bell	:	common decorative motif used in temple pillars and other elements
Chauhans	:	see, Chahamana
chaumukha darwaza	:	four-faced gate, that is, having four openings, one on each side
chhajja	:	projection supported on brackets or struts above door, wall, arch, etc.
chhatri	:	a pillared pavilion; small domed turret; the term is also used for cenotaphs or funerary monuments particularly in Rajasthan
dargah	:	a royal court, precinct. Term used for a Muslim shrine or tomb of some reputed holy person, and which is the object of pilgrimage and adoration
darwaza	:	door, doorway, gate or portal
Deliwals	:	also called Dehliwal or Jital. Billon (alloy of gold and silver) coin of the early Sultanate period. It weighed usually between 3.2 and 3.5 g. The three minting places were Delhi, Lahore, and Badaun.
Ganesha	:	lord of the *ganas*, attendants of the god Siva. He is the son of Siva and Parvati. Elephant-headed, he removes obstacles and is invoked invariably before commencing any religious rites or ritual.

Garuda	:	eagle or mythic sun-bird who is Vishnu's mount
ghata-pallava	:	vase-and-foliage. A motif commonly used in temples
Gupta	:	a dynasty that ruled over large parts of India between early fourth and early sixth centuries. Their capital was Pataliputra, modern Patna, in Bihar.
Gupta script	:	style, form or shape of alphabets of Brahmi script in use during Gupta period and later up to the eighth century. Called box-headed, it is generally characterized by square and triangular head marks.
hauz	:	a pond or tank; also called *haud*
haveli	:	large building complex for residence with suites around one or more open courts. Mansion, merchant's house.
Hijri	:	also Hijrah or Hijra. Literally 'migration'. The migration of the Prophet Muhammad from Mecca to Medina. Muhammadan era commencing from 15 July 622
horseshoe arch	:	arch having the form of a horseshoe
Jahanara	:	elder daughter of the Mughal emperor Shah Jahan. She died in 1681 and is buried in the Nizamuddin Dargah complex in Delhi. Her grave is simple and without any cover since she wished that 'Let naught cover my grave save the green grass/For grass well suffices as a covering for the grave of the lowly'.
Jain	:	followers of the spiritual path initiated by twenty-four Tirthankaras of whom Rishabhadeva was the first and Mahavira, an elder contemporary of Buddha, was the last.
jaali	:	perforated or filigree-patterned screen, mostly of stone or wood, having different designs, used on windows or within pillars. Some of the jaalis are very artistically executed and are of great aesthetic merit.
Jami' Masjid	:	large congregational mosque where the *khutbah* or Friday oration is delivered
Jantar Mantar	:	complex with special masonry structures for use in astronomical observations. Corrupt form of

		Sanskrit *yantra* (instrument) and mantra (formula or incantation)
Jogamaya	:	Sanskrit, Yoga-Maya. Mystic female divinity connected with worship of the goddess. Divine female
kabutar-khana	:	pigeon-house
Khandavaprastha	:	mentioned in the Mahabharata as the place located on the bank of the Yamuna which was given by Dhritarashtra to the Pandavas
Khan-i-Khanan	:	Khan of Khans, i.e., the greatest Khan. A title
kirttimukha	:	'face of glory'. Protective motif used in decoration; grotesque mask as a protector of worshipper from evil
kos-minar	:	masonry pillars erected along the Grand Trunk Road and other main roads of the Mughal empire as indicators of distance like modern milestones. These pillars are circular or polygonal in shape and form and are usually about 5–7 m (16.04–22.96 feet) high so as to be visible from a distance. A *kos* is about 3.21 km (2 miles). It is also mentioned there are 5000 *gaz* or yards to a kos which works out to 457.2 m. Some scholars also suggest that in ancient times one kos was equal to 9 miles or 14.484 km.
Krishna	:	eighth incarnation of Vishnu; the cowherd god
Kufic	:	ancient characters of Arabic writing named after al-Kufah, a city on the western bank of the river Euphrates. Kufic Arabic letters are square and heavy. Ancient copies of the Quran are written in Kufic
Kushan	:	also spelt Kushana. Central Asian tribe which ruled over large parts of north India between first and third centuries CE
measuring rod	:	a yard, that is, a *gaj* which was used as a standard measure by masons
mihrab	:	niche in the centre of the wall of a mosque which marks the direction of Mecca. Walls of some tombs also have a *mihrab* in the same direction
minar	:	properly *manarah*, from *manar*, 'a place where a fire is lit, lighthouse, pillar'. The lofty turret of a mosque

from which the *muezzin* or 'caller to prayer' invites the people to prayer

mimbar : also *minbar*. Pulpit in a mosque from which the *khutbah* or sermon is recited

Modhera : town in Gujarat famous for its Sun Temple

mu'azzin : (also spelt *mu'ezzin*) The caller of the *azaan* or the summons to prayer (muezzin in English)

mutavalli : (also spelt *mutawalli*) Lit. 'a person endowed with authority'. The trustee or superintendent of a mosque

Naskh/Naskhi : calligraphic style of Arabic writing, with round characters. Style generally employed in manuscripts and derived from *naskh* or *nuskhah*, 'copy'

ogee-shaped arch : moulding of an arch having a convex and concave curve; S-shaped

Om : sacred or mystic syllable

Painted Grey Ware : abbrev. PGW. Typical pottery of grey colour having simple decoration painted mainly in black, though sometimes in red as well. It has a well-defined spatial distribution, particularly in the Ganga-Yamuna doab and parts of Rajasthan and is generally placed in the first half of the first millennium BCE

Palam *baoli* inscription : inscription engraved on a stone slab originally fixed in the baoli or step-well at Palam village, close to the Delhi airport. The inscription, dated Vikrama Samvat 1333 (1276 CE), gives the name and family details of the person who had built the stepwell.

Pandavas : sons of Pandu, the ruler of Hastinapura

Parshvanatha : twenty-third Jaina Tirthankara. His cognizance is snake

Parshvanatha-charitra : written in Vikrama Samvat 1189 (1132 CE) by poet Shridhara

pattavalis : lists of Jaina teacher-disciples

pendentive : triangular, curved overhanging surface by means of which a (circular) dome is supported on a square or polygonal compartment

Phoolwalon ki Sair : Sair-i-Gulfaroshan, flower-vendors' fair, started during the time of Mughal emperor Akbar II (1806–37). Flower-bedecked large fans are presented by flower-vendors at the dargah of Qutb Sahib and the Jogamaya temple. The procession starts from Jharna, the overflow outlet of the Hauz-i-Shamsi.

Pratiharas
: dynasty which ruled over large parts of north India from about the second quarter of the eighth century for more than 100 years

Prithviraja-raso
: a poetic composition on Prithviraja Chauhan in old Hindi by Chand Bardai composed sometime in the twelfth century

Raushanara
: younger daughter of Mughal emperor Shah Jahan. She died in 1671. She built for herself a garden-tomb in 1650 in Delhi. Called Raushanara Bagh, it is located in north Delhi.

Rishabhanatha
: the first among the 24 Jaina Tirthankaras. Also called Adinatha. His cognizances are bull and *dharma-chakra*.

Shaka
: Sanskritized name for Scythians, originally a tribe of Central Asian nomads who ruled over parts of north-western and western India between the first century BCE and second century CE. Shaka era, starting from 78 CE, is also ascribed by some scholars to them.

Samvat
: meaning 'year'. Era dating from 57 BCE. Also called *Samvatsara* or Vikrama Samvat

sarai
: also spelt serai. Caravanserai built along the main roads for travellers, merchants, etc. Large sarais were built along the Grand Trunk Road following an almost identical plan. These are impressive structures with adequate arrangements for the safety and other needs of the merchants.

squinch arch
: arch placed diagonally at internal angles of a square room in the phase of transition to convert it from square to octagon to support the circular dome. An arch carried across the corner of a room under a superimposed mass

Shridhara
: author of poetic work entitled *Parshvanatha-charitra* composed in Vikrama Samvat 1189 (1132 CE)

stalactite pendentive	:	ornament resembling the formation of calcium carbonate hanging from the roof or walls of a cavern; appears to have originated in the multiplication of small squinch arches on a pendentive, hence stalactite pendentive. Arabic *muqarna*
Sultanate	:	includes Delhi Sultanate (1206–1526 CE) during which five dynasties, Slave or Mamluk, Khalji, Tughluq, Sayyid, and Lodi, ruled from Delhi
Sun temple at Modhera	:	temple at Modhera, district Mahesana in Gujarat, dedicated to Surya or the Sun-god. Dating from 1026 CE, the temple is assigned to the reign of Bhima I (1024–66 CE), the Solanki king
Shunga	:	dynasty which followed the Mauryas in about 187 BCE and continued to rule till about 75 BCE
Surahs	:	lit. 'a row or series'. Term used exclusively for chapters of the Quran; these are 114 in number
Tirthankara	:	Being who has attained perfection of knowledge, speech, worship, and absolute security. One who finds a ford (*tirtha*) through this world (*samsara*); one who forms four communities (*tirtha*) of monks and nuns and male and female lay followers
Tomars	:	family of Rajputs who ruled over Delhi from the tenth century onwards before the Chahamanas or Chauhans. According to tradition, Tomar ruler Anangpal is credited with the founding of Delhi.
Vikrama *Samvat*	:	abbre. VS. Era beginning from 57 BCE
Vigraharaja	:	king Vigraharaja IV (c. 1153–64 CE) also known as Visaladeva or Bisaldeo of the Chahamana dynasty of Shakambhari in Rajasthan. He captured Delhi from the Tomars.
Vishnu	:	one of the principal Hindu deities; 'the preserver'
Vishnu-*dhvaja*	:	flagstaff of Vishnu
voussoirs	:	each of the wedge-shaped or tapered stones forming an arch
Yogamaya	:	name of Durga; the inaccessible or terrific goddess; *maya* or magical power of abstract meditation. Popularly called Jogamaya

yoginis   : female divinities who are manifestations or companions of the Great Goddess; a female endowed with magical power. *Yoginis* enumerated number 8, 64, 65, and 81.

Zil Qada   : (*Zu'l-Qa'dah*) The eleventh month of the Muslim year. It was the month in which the ancient Arabs abstained from warfare and the people were engaged in peaceful works.

Further Reading

Anantharaman, T.R., *The Rustless Wonder—A Study of Delhi Iron Pillar*, Vigyan Prasar, New Delhi, 1997.

Asher, Frederick M. and G.S. Gai (eds), *Indian Epigraphy: Its Bearing on the History of Art*, Oxford & IBH Publishing Co. and American Institute of Indian Studies, New Delhi, 1985.

Balasubramaniam, R., *Delhi Iron Pillar: New Insights*, Indian Institute of Advanced Study, Shimla, and Aryan Books International, New Delhi, 2002.

____, 'Influence of Manufacturing Methodology on the Corrosion Resistance of the Delhi Iron Pillar', *Indian Journal of History of Science*, 38(3), pp. 195–213.

____, *The World Heritage Complex of the Qutub*, Aryan Books International, New Delhi, 2005.

Balasubramaniam, R. and Meera I. Dass, 'On the Astronomical Significance of the Delhi Iron Pillar', *Current Science*, 86(8), 25 April 2004, pp. 1,134–42.

Begley, W.E., *Monumental Islamic Calligraphy from India*, with a preface by Z.A. Desai, Islamic Foundation, Villa Park, Illinois, 1985.

Bhandarkar, Devadatta Ramakrishna, Bahadurchand Chhabra, and G.S. Gai (eds.), *Inscriptions of the Early Gupta Kings*, Corpus Inscriptionum Indicarum, vol. III, Archaeological Survey of India, New Delhi, 1981, pp. 257–9.

Brown, Percy, *Indian Architecture: The Islamic Period*, Taraporevala's Treasure House of Books, 5th edn, Bombay, 1968.

Cole, H.H., *Architecture of Ancient Delhi: Especially the Buildings Around the Kutb Minar*, London, 1872.

Cunningham, Alexander, *Archaeological Survey of India, Four Reports Made during the Years 1862–63–64–65*, Simla, 1871, vol. I, pp. 132–231. Reprinted by Archaeological Survey of India, New Delhi, 2000.

———, *Archaeological Survey of India,Reports for the year 1871, Delhi by J.D. Beglar, Agra by A.C.L. Carllyle*, Calcutta, 1874, vol. IV, pp. 1–91. Reprinted by Archaeological Survey of India, New Delhi, 2000.

———, *Archaeological Survey of India, Report of a Tour in Eastern Rajputana in 1882–83*, Calcutta, 1885, vol. XX, pp. 142–61. Reprinted by Archeological Survey of India, New Delhi, 2000.

Desai, Z.A., 'Islamic inscriptions: Their bearing on monuments', in Asher and Gai, *Indian Epigraphy*, pp. 251–6.

Dvivedi, Hariharniwas, *Dilli ke Tomar 736–1193 Isvi (Tomars of Delhi AD 736–1193*, in Hindi), Vidya Mandir Prakashan, Murar, Gwalior, 1973.

Fanshawe, H.C., *Delhi Past and Present*, London, 1902. Reprinted by Aryan Books International, New Delhi, 2002.

Fergusson, James, *History of Indian and Eastern Architecture*, John Murray, London, 1910, vol. II. Reprinted by Munshiram Manoharlal, Delhi, 1967.

Frykenberg, R.E. (ed.), *Delhi through the Ages: Essays in Urban History, Culture and Society*, Oxford University Press, New Delhi, 1986.

Ghosh, A. (ed.), *Jaina Art and Architecture: Published on the Occasion of the 2,500th Anniversary of Tirthankara Mahavira*, 3 vols, Bharatiya Jnanapith, New Delhi, 1975.

Ghosh, M.K., 'The Delhi Iron Pillar and its Iron', *NML Technical Journal*, vol. 5, 1963, pp. 31–45.

Hodfield, R., 'Sinhalese Iron and Steel of Ancient Origin', *Journal of Iron and Steel Institute*, 85, 1912, pp. 134–74.

Hearn, G.R., *The Seven Cities of Delhi*, London, 1906.

Hillenbrand, Robert, *Islamic Architecture: Form, Function and Meaning*, Edinburgh University Press, Edinburgh, 1994.

Horowitz, J., 'The Inscriptions of Muhammad ibn Sam, Qutbuddin Aibeg and Iltutmish', *Epigraphia Indo-Moslemica*, 1911–12, pp. 12–34.

Husain, Maulvi Muhammad Ashraf, *A Record of all the Quranic and Non-Historical Epigraphs on the Protected Monuments in the Delhi Province*, Memoirs of the Archaeological Survey of India, No. 47, Central Publication Branch, Calcutta, 1936, reprinted by Archaeological Survey of India, New Delhi, 1999.

Joshi, Jagat Pati, Krishna Deva *et al.*, *Inventory of Monuments and Sites of National Importance*, 1(3), Delhi Circle, Archaeological Survey of India, New Delhi, 2004.

Joshi, M.C., 'Some Nagari Inscriptions on the Qutb Minar', in *Medieval India: A Miscellany*, Centre of Advanced Studies, Department of History, Aligarh Muslim University, Aligarh, 1972, pp. 3–7.

Joshi, M.C., and S.K. Gupta (eds.), *King Chandra and the Mehrauli Pillar*, Kusumanjali Prakashan, Meerut, 1989.

Joshi, M.C., S.K. Gupta, and Shankar Goyal (eds.), *The Delhi Iron Pillar: Its Art, Metallurgy and Inscriptions*, Kusumanjali Prakashan, Jodhpur, 1996.

Joshi, M.C., and B.M. Pande, 'A Newly Discovered Inscription of Asoka at Bahapur, Delhi', *Journal of the Asiatic Society*, London, October 1967, pp. 96–8.

Kaye, M.M. (ed.), *The Golden Calm: An English Lady's Life in Moghul Delhi—Reminiscences by Emily, Lady Clive Bayley and by her Father, Sir Thomas Metcalfe*, The Viking Press, New York, 1980.

Keene, H.G., *Handbook for Visitors to Delhi*, rewritten by E.A. Duncan, Calcutta, 1906.

Khan, Sayyid Ahmad, *Athar-al-Sanadid*, Delhi, 1847 and Cawnpore 1907. Edited by Khaliq Anjum and reprinted by Urdu Academy, Delhi, 2000.

Lewis, Karoki (Photographs) and Charles Lewis (Text), *Mehrauli: A View from the Qutb*, Foundation Books, Harper Collins, New Delhi.

Mani, B.R., *Delhi—Threshold of the Orient: Studies in Archaeological Investigations*, Aryan Books International, New Delhi, 1997.

Mujeeb, Muhammad, 'The Qutb Complex as a Social Document', in *Islamic Influence on Indian Society*, Meenakshi Prakashan, Delhi, 1972, pp. 114–27. Also reprinted in Monica Juneja (ed.), *Architecture in Medieval India: Forms, Context, Histories*, Permanent Black, Delhi, 2001, pp. 290–300.

Nath, R., *History of Sultanate Architecture*, Abhinav Publications, New Delhi, 1978.

———, *Monuments of Delhi: Historical Study*, Ambika Publications and Indian Institute of Islamic Studies, New Delhi, 1979. This is a translation of some portions from Sir Sayyid Ahmad Khan's *Athar-us-Sanadid* with reproductions of some select illustrations.

———, *Jharokha: An Illustrated Glossary of Indo-Muslim Architecture*, The Historical Research Documentation Programme, Jaipur, 1986.

Nanda, Ratish *et al.* (compilers), *Delhi: The Built Heritage, A Listing*, Indian National Trust for Art and Cultural Heritage, Delhi Chapter, vol. 2, pp. 219–343.

Page, J.A., *An Historical Memoir on the Qutb: Delhi*, Memoirs of the

Archaeological Survey of India, No. 22, Archeological Survey of India, New Delhi, 1926. Reprinted by Archaeological Survey of India, New Delhi, 1998.

Page, J.A., *Guide to the Qutb, Delhi*, Manager of Publications, Delhi, 1938.

Page, J.A. and Y.D. Sharma, *Qutb Minar & Adjoining Monuments*, Archaeological Survey of India, New Delhi, 2002.

Page, J. Burton, 'Dihli', in C.E. Bosworth *et al.* (eds), *Encyclopaedia of Islam*, 2nd edn, vol. 2, pp. 255–66.

Pande, B.M., 'A Late Acheulian Handaxe from New Delhi', *Man and Environment*, vol. IX, pp. 157–8.

Pereira, José, *The Sacred Architecture of Islam*, Aryan Books International, New Delhi, 2004.

Prasad, Pushpa, *Sanskrit Inscriptions of Delhi Sultanate 1191–1526*, Centre of Advanced Study in History, Aligarh Muslim University, Oxford University Press, New Delhi, 1990.

Sengupta, R., 'The Qutb Minar: Strengthening the foundations', *Puratattva*, Bulletin of the Indian Archaeological Society, No. 10, 1978–9, pp. 72–5.

Sharma, A.K., *Prehistoric Delhi and its Neighbourhood*, Aryan Books International, New Delhi, 1993.

Sharma, Y.D., *Delhi and its Neighbourhood*, Archaeological Survey of India, New Delhi, 1964. There are several editions and reprints of this book, the latest being the reprint of 2001.

Smith, R.V., *The Delhi that No One Knows*, Chronicle Books, an imprint of DC Publishers, New Delhi, 2005.

Spear, T.G.P., *Delhi: Its Monuments and History*, updated and annotated by Narayani Gupta and Laura Sykes, Oxford University Press, New Delhi, 1994.

Stephen, Carr, *The Archaeology and Monumental Remains of Delhi*, Mission Press, Ludhiana and Calcutta, 1876. Reprinted by Aryan Books International, New Delhi, 2002 with photographs, lithographs and aquatints.

Singh, Upinder, *Ancient Delhi*, Oxford University Press, New Delhi, 1999.

Sunil Kumar, 'Qutb in Modern Memory', in his *The Present in Delhi's Pasts*, Three Essays, New Delhi, 2002.

Tadgell, Christopher, *The History of Architecture in India: From the Dawn of Civilization to the End of the Raj*, Architecture Design and Technology Press, London, 1990.

Thapar, B.K., 'The Buried Past of Delhi', *Expedition*, 14(1), 1972, pp. 21–6.

———, *Recent Archaeological Discoveries in India*, UNESCO, The Centre for East Asian Cultural Studies, Tokyo, 1985, pp. 132–5.

Trivedi, Mudit, *The Archaeology of Delhi*, Perspective from a Survey of the Jawaharlal Nehru [University] Campus, paper presented at the seminar 'Ancient India' New Research, 27–8 August 2005 organized by Manána, Delhi.

Welch, Anthony, 'Qur'an and Tomb: The religious Epigraphs of Two Early Sultanate Tombs in Delhi', in Asher and Gai, *Indian Epigraphy*, pp. 257–67.

Yamamoto, Tatsuro, Matsuo Ara, and Tokifusa Tsukinowa, *Delhi: Architectural Remains of the Delhi Sultanate Period*, 3 vols, Tokyo, 1968–70.

Yazdani, G., 'Inscriptions of the Khalji Sultans of Delhi and their contemporaries in Bengal', *Epigraphia Indo-Moslemica*, 1917–18, pp. 23–30.

Zafar Hasan (compiler), *Delhi Province: List of Muhammadan and Hindu Monuments*, vol. III, *Mehrauli Zail*, Superintendent Government Printing, Calcutta, 1922, pp. 1–87. Reprinted under the title *Monuments of Delhi: Lasting Splendour of the Great Mughals and Others*, Aryan Books International, New Delhi, 1997.